It's O.K. - This is Church

Steven B. Schafer

25th Year Publications
© 2007 Steven B. Schafer
ISBN: 978-0-6151-4869-4

Dedicated to all the wonderful people of the Mt. Hope Congregational Church who have listened to good sermons and bad - who always complimented the good and allowed the bad to dissipate in the wind.

Preface

I've been at the same church for 25 years. Over the course of those years I've delivered more than 1100 sermons and I can only remember two or three myself. I don't really expect my congregation to remember any of them for more than a day or so. And that's OK because I've always held that it isn't the individual sermon that is important, but rather the whole scheme of things – how teaching after teaching, inspiration after inspiration, lesson after lesson all comes together to impact one's life. And, I've got to say, if the people I see when I look out from the pulpit on a Sunday morning have become the people they are, in any small way, due to my sermons, I'm doing something right. I've got a truly wonderful congregation.

Several from my congregation have asked me, over the years, to put some of my sermons into book form. I resisted for a long time, not being able to imagine anyone wanting to read sermons. There is a great difference between hearing a work written to be heard and reading those same words in the silence of one's own mind. A sermon, read, doesn't always flow as smoothly as the written word should and therefore, sometimes, seems disjointed. But that is the way we actually speak and hear and thus the way sermons are written. I hope that, having to read instead of hear won't be too off-putting.

I made a deal with those who wanted a bound series of sermons. I told them that if they could come up with some sermons that meant something to them over the years, I'd put a book together.

I was astounded. Some of the requested sermons were delivered as much as 15 years ago! And only one of them, of all those suggested, would I have chosen, myself, as one of the best or most significant (I'll let you decide for yourself which one that might be). I believe that means that the Holy Spirit works in lives apart from our weak wisdom... If a word or a phrase or a whole sermon speaks to you from this collection, may our God receive all the praise and glory.

Rev. Steven Schafer has been the pastor of the Mt. Hope Congregational Church of Livonia, MI since 1982.

Contents

IT'S OK... THIS IS CHURCH — 7
May 2, 1993. Revised and delivered again on April 28, 2002.
Requested by Spencer Rife

MENDING BROKEN RELATIONSHIPS — 13
September 19, 1993
Requested by Spencer Rife

WHAT DOES JESUS EXPECT? — 17
Requested by Spencer Rife

YOU'VE GOT TO HAVE A DREAM — 23
October 31, 1993
Requested by "Anonymous"

THE DREAMER — 29
January 9, 1994
Requested by Spencer Rife

IS MATTER ALL THAT MATTERS? — 33
February 20, 1994
Requested by Spencer Rife

INTENTIONAL FRIENDS — 37
April 2, 1995
Requested by Sue Schafer

SAND CASTLES — 43
September 24, 1995
Requested by Cheryl Myatt

FIVE TALENT PEOPLE — 49
November 5, 1995
Requested by Spencer Rife

SEEING THE BEAUTY IN OTHERS — 55
    March 12, 2000
    Requested by Mary Orselli

WHY THEY HATE US —
AND WHAT WE CAN DO ABOUT IT — 61
    September 15, 2002
    Requested by Margaret Holden

THE CHURCH IN AMERICA — 67
    September 7, 2003
    Requested by Sue Schafer

WHOSE FRIES ARE THESE, ANYWAY — 73
    November 16, 2003
    Requested by Heidi Schmitt

SMALL TALK — 79
    November 21, 2004
    Requested by Glen Lundgren

BELIEVE WHATEVER YOU WANT — 85
    November 20, 2005
    Requested by Spencer Rife

DO THE LOVING THING — 91
    January 8, 2006
    Requested by "Anonymous"

CHRISTMAS B.C. — THE SEED — 97
    December 3, 2006
    Requested by Sue Hannis

IT'S OK... THIS IS CHURCH

Isaiah 52:7-12 and Acts 2: 42-47.

They devoted themselves to the apostles' teaching and to the fellowship, to the breaking of bread and to prayer.

Acts 2:42

There is one time of my week that I absolutely LOVE being at Mt. Hope. Don't get me wrong – I love my job. I love this church. I love all the people who come here. But from 7:15 on Wednesday evenings until about 7:45 I experience nothing but joy. Songs and Silence ends at 7:15 (a wonderful, prayerful experience that is coming to an end this Wednesday for the summer – I hope many of you will plan to join us in the fall), but the Pioneer Clubs haven't dismissed yet. When I can, I go into the Fellowship Hall or the back hallway and see all the parents waiting for their children to come out of the classrooms. I look at all those young parents and I fall in love with every one of them. They want the very best for their children. They love God. They love one another... I love listening to their interactions... Then the kids start coming out. What a joy! Children of all ages having experienced FUN in church! They come out showing what they've made or giggling when they see mom or dad. They are maybe holding hands or talking to one another... I love to chat with them a little bit. These little ones make me happy. They make my day...

Children grow up. They become adults. On the way they experience all kinds of things which build their self-confidence and often things which tear it down. I hope Mt. Hope will always be remembered as a place that built it up... Those who experience more of the positive and less of the negative end up being self-assured, confident, out-going achievers in life... But those who are constantly put down, are often destined to remain that way all their lives... It is SO important to encourage and build up children...

You know, one of the best places for the building of self-esteem is right here in church. It's true. I often feel bad that parents don't take their children to church. Even if it weren't for the spiritual things kids get at church (a sense of right and wrong – of good and bad – of God and His greatness...), the church has no rival when it comes to affirming a child's value. Where else can a kid run up and down the halls and see smiles on adult faces as they chat with one another (and, sometimes, a surrogate parent telling them to slow down)? Where else can a kid go where so many adults act like extended family and call him/her by name? Where else will no one let you get hurt nor will they let you get away with something you shouldn't be doing? Where else can a kid feel a part of something a lot bigger than themselves – something as adult and grand as worship – by coming up for the children's sermon and taking part – by singing hymns standing right beside mom and dad, doing the same thing they are doing – or doing something as sacred as eating and drinking the body and blood of Jesus Christ?

This was all dramatically brought to my attention a few years ago when we started our acolyte program where the kids light the candles at the beginning of worship... One little girl was doing it for the first time and was a bit nervous. The usher who helped light her candle lighter tried to assure her that she would do just fine. She took the lighter and, as she headed down the aisle for the first time, she said to him, "It's OK if I make a mistake. This is church..."

Our lesson from the book of Acts gives us a glimpse of a church filled with people who have discovered that wonderful principle... – It's OK if I make a mistake... it's OK to be who I am... it's OK to be 'on the path' but not having yet arrived... This is church...

In that first church that began nearly 2000 years ago, there was a sense of excitement, of love and purpose. They ate together and worshipped together. The learned together. They experienced unity. And the results were truly amazing. "And day by day the Lord added to their number... "

Wouldn't it be great to recapture the enthusiasm and energy of that early church? Wouldn't it be great to have that same kind of love and harmony? I think maybe we can. Let's look at some of the things that made that first church so alive, so powerful.

We discover, first of all, that **THE TEACHING MINISTRY OF THE EARLY CHURCH WAS VERY IMPORTANT.** After work each evening the believers would gather at someone's home and share a meal. They would sing hymns and offer prayers thanking God for all their many blessings. And they would listen to the apostles teach. And through their regular meetings together, they grew in their love and affirmation of one another... They had found that the relationship they shared with Christ drew them together in a powerful way like nothing else could have done. As they learned about Jesus and talked about their experience with Him in their own lives, they grew spiritually and began to see themselves as family. They began to see the church as a secure place – as a "home" – as a refuge – as a "sanctuary" – such that now, as they took the message of relationship with Jesus throughout the world, they could always come back and be loved... even if the rest of the world showed them no love... HERE they were always loved...

There is a story about Admiral Byrd, the famous explorer. It seems that he once found himself about 100 yards away from the safety of his South Pole shelter when a blizzard hit. The temperature was way below zero, and the snow made everything a blinding white. There were no landmarks available to give him a clue as to where he was or needed to be... He knew that if he didn't find the comparative warmth and safety in a relatively short time, he would freeze to death.

Admiral Byrd couldn't see his hut or anything else in the freezing blizzard that would guide him to safety. He knew that he would freeze to death if he didn't find the shelter of his hut quickly. He also knew that if he struck out blindly, without a central reference point for a sense of direction, he would become hopelessly lost. Refusing to panic, the admiral assessed the situation. In his hand was a 10-foot pole that he carried with him to probe for holes in the ice as he walked. He stuck the pole in the snow and tied his bright-colored scarf to it. Then he began looking for the hut, keeping the pole in sight as a central reference point, knowing that he could always return to it if necessary.

He struck out, first in one direction, then in another, always keeping the pole and scarf in sight. Three times he came back to his point of reference; on the fourth try, he found his shelter. His life was saved.

Hopefully, none of us will ever find ourselves in the same kind of situation... But aren't there many times in your life when a crisis occurs; when you just don't know which way to turn? At those times, you need a point of reference; a sense of direction. It comes through knowing Christ – it comes through reading the Bible – it comes through being a part of the body of Christ – the church. The strength of the church is that it has a set of standards and teachings that have stood the test of time... It's not that the application isn't constantly changing as the world changes – it does – but the basic precepts have guided people into positive and loving and gracious living for centuries... There can be no greater security than that...

THAT FIRST CHURCH WAS ALSO A PRAYING CHURCH. They thanked God daily for all their many blessings and for the opportunity for fellowship and learning together. I often wonder what would happen in our church if everyone agreed to pray daily for our church family? I know everyone says how much they appreciate the cards they receive when they are sick. That's a wonderful ministry that many of you have undertaken. But do you pray as you send the card? I hope so. I hope getting a card when you are ill is the same as knowing that person has been praying for you... Do you pray each day for the church as a whole, for the pastor, for Shari and Jessica and your deacon and the Trustees and the other church leaders and the ushers and Sunday School teachers? Do you pray for visitors – those who have visited us and those who **will** visit us? Do you pray for the missionaries we support? Do you pray for the little girl our Sunday School children are helping? Do you pray for our city and our nation and our world? Do you pray for wisdom and unity in our congregation? The early church did great things and saw tremendous results because they were a praying church... (and of course they then went out and did the things that influenced what they prayed about)...

I think that all of us generally need to pray more... And I am confident that if we do, great things will happen. Pray more. Set aside some time each day to spend just talking with God.

So – the church of the New Testament was a church centered on teaching and on praying and on fellowship. We also discover that **THE EARLY CHURCH THRIVED BECAUSE IT KNEW HOW TO SHARE.**

"They would sell their possessions and goods," says Luke, "and distribute the proceeds to all, as any had need."

Generosity – giving – sacrificing to give... Those aren't comfortable concepts for most people. But in the church, that is the wisdom. Only in giving – only in sharing what we have with others – only in going beyond what is comfortable to give – are we truly blessed... Only in giving what we have are we able to overcome the worlds pull toward worshipping material goods and money...

In the Old Testament, believers were required to give a "tithe" (10%) of their income. But the New Testament church saw that as being rather artificial. Tithing is not enough, they taught. ALL OF IT belongs to God. You can give 10% to the church if you want to, but you MUST remember that EVERYTHING WE HAVE belongs to God and not us and we must use all things as good stewards...

The saddest people in this world are people who never discover the joy of giving. The church thrives when it knows how to share; when it is willing to sacrifice to help others. Every year, it seems, there is some kind of natural disaster somewhere in the world. Governments pitch in sometimes with aid... but almost always churches and church sponsored organizations are at the forefront... Christians are the first to reach out to assist in crisis...

That's the reason the church is the special place it is. That's why it's OK if you make a mistake. The church is a family. It is a unique place where people grow to love one another and affirm one another's worth. It is a place for learning of righteousness and values unlike any other. It is a place for prayer – a place where the very power of God is utilized... It is a place where people share – of themselves and of their resources that others might come in and learn real love – the love of a Christ who came and taught and prayed and shared that we might live forever.

You don't have to be perfect to be here. "It's OK if you make a mistake. This is Church."

MENDING BROKEN RELATIONSHIPS

Ezekiel 33:7-9 and Matthew 18:15-2

"If your brother sins against you, go and show him his fault, just between the two of you. If he listens to you, you have won your brother over. But if he will not listen, take one or two others along, so that 'every matter may be established by the testimony of two or three witnesses.' If he refuses to listen to them, tell it to the church..."

Matthew 18:15-17

I believe that personal relationships are perhaps the most important aspect of human life... yet we take them for granted more than almost anything else. We do less to maintain them than we do a car or boat or even a vacuum cleaner. A recent study indicated that, in America, only one man in five has a real friend. ONE IN FIVE! I don't know what the statistic for women are, but look around you this morning. Statistically only 20% of the men have a close friend. I hope that statistic does not hold true within the church. In the church we have a unique thing going. What the world needs and doesn't seem able to supply, we have. We try to "major" in relationships. That's what goes on in baptisms and marriages and fellowship groups and Sunday School classes – and even as we conduct funerals... commemorating – remembering relationships...

Fellowship and relationship are our primary tasks as Christians. Jesus called the church together to be a caring community... to reach out arms of sympathy and support to those who are in distress. To rejoice with those who rejoice and to weep with those who weep. Kahlil Gibran once remarked that "we can forget those with whom we have laughed, but we can never forget those with whom we have cried"... Millions of people – most of us sitting here this morning – have felt the support of the Christian community in times of crisis in our lives...

The scripture passage we read from Matthew a few minutes ago is perhaps one of the most important passages in the New Testament about relationships – specifically about *broken* relationships. What Jesus is saying here is "If anyone sins against you, you must *spare no effort* to be reconciled to that person again." He is saying that, as Christians, we must not tolerate any situation in which there is a breach of personal relationship between us and another member of the community. To allow such a thing will weaken the whole body.

But Jesus isn't just a philosopher. He gives us some very specific steps to take (and I don't think these are useful just for conflicts with other Christians, but perhaps in all relationships – at work, with children, with spouses, with neighbors...)

1) If we feel that someone has wronged us, we should immediately put our complaint into words. There is *nothing* worse than allowing a bad feeling to eat away at you inside. That can poison your mind and your heart and ultimately your whole life. You've seen it happen to people. They have such resentment or hatred inside that it affects their very personality. Sometimes it may even cause physical problems... But they never realize that the person they feel so strongly about probably doesn't even know they are so upset. They *only hurt themselves*. STEP ONE: Bring it out in the open. State the problem in words out loud to someone. Many times you will find that just saying it will show how unimportant or trivial the issue really is.

Whenever I have a bride that is getting really up-tight about all the details that need yet to be done before the big day I ask her to list for me what they are. Then I ask her to tell me what is the worse thing that could possibly happen if each one didn't get done at all... The perspective of stating the situation out loud almost always brings a new sense of calm. She can see that these things are frills and are nice to have but if not – no big deal.

The same is true with conflict. When it is stated out loud it is often so insignificant that it immediately melts away...

2) Jesus gives us a second step to take if the first one doesn't resolve the problem. If we think someone has wronged us, we should go to see him/her personally. More trouble has been caused by the writing of letters than by almost anything else, in terms of relationships. A letter can be misread and misunderstood; it can convey a tone or an attitude

that it was never meant to. If we have a difference with someone, there is only one way to settle it – and that is face to face

Myron Augsberger wrote a little book titled, "Caring Enough To Confront." You don't even have to read the book to know what it is about. It is about confronting others when you have a problem with something. It maintains that confronting a situation is what Jesus always did... that it is, in reality, the loving, Christian approach to take. It is "so much easier to just bury it somewhere inside and never have confrontations with people – you just will avoid them... Confrontations can cause arguments or hurt feelings – and that is never comfortable – but *not* confronting can destroy the relationship – maybe forever

3) Step three. If verbalizing the problem doesn't help. And if approaching the person gently and in love doesn't help, then we should find some kind and wise and gracious third party to act as a reconciler (this idea goes all the way back to the book of Deuteronomy – it's not new with Jesus). Be well aware that this person, if truly wise, may find that it is *us* that is at fault as much – or instead of – the other person.

There is something uniquely helpful about talking out a problem between two people with a third person present. A new atmosphere develops and there is a *chance* that each of us can see ourselves "as others see us." That's the genius behind modern psychological counseling. The secular world has discovered something Jesus said a long time ago – that even Jesus got from the scriptures long before his time... get together with someone who can help clarify the issues and wonders can be worked.

4) Suppose that even this fails. Jesus suggests that this is the time to take the issue before the Christian fellowship. Why? Because the Christian fellowship is one which ought to be involved in prayer and love and brimming over with "right" relationships. If the fellowship of believers, gathered in love, praying, cannot help save your relationship, maybe it can't be saved.

I don't know exactly how this works out in practical terms. I don't think Jesus is suggesting that the church act as a kind of "court" to make judgments as to guilt and innocence of those in conflict. I think he must be suggesting that there is tremendous power in prayer and that if you are ready to make the broken relationship so public that you request prayer of the church, powerful things can happen (but, of course, this is *after* you've gone through the previous steps). In fact, this passage ends with the strange teaching that if two or more agree on any particular prayer, you will get an answer. That isn't some kind of magic formula. It is suggesting that God's answer to the Christian's prayer, if prayed in the proper attitude, will be answered in the best possible way – in accordance with the wisdom and working of God (which, of course, *is* the proper attitude – "thy will be done").

Now comes the most difficult part of the passage: If you've verbalized the problem – said it out loud – and nothing changes... If you've gone to the person with whom you have the problem and nothing is resolved... If you get some counseling help that doesn't help... If you have sought the prayers of the church but they have been of no avail... The final step is: Think of that other person as a Gentile or as a tax collector.

Now, if you were Jewish in Jesus' day, you would have nothing to do with a Gentile (someone who is not Jewish). They were like eating pork – unclean. And tax collectors – well, they haven't changed all that much in 2000 years. Everyone still wants to avoid them as much as possible.

Most people would think that Jesus is saying that at this point you've done all you can and it is now OK just to "write them off". And if anyone else said, "Consider them as Gentiles and tax-collectors" that would be absolutely true. But this is Jesus speaking here. Jesus *never wrote anybody off.* Jesus was accused of being a *friend* of tax-collectors and "sinners" (another word for Gentiles). Jesus is saying that maybe your conflict can't be resolved. But if not, put it aside. Forget about it. Be a friend despite what has happened... and who knows... And in doing that we can demonstrate the very best of Christian love. If we can be injured and seek reconciliation without success and *still* love that person who injured us, we know something about the love of God, for ultimately, that is what happens between us and him. Even though we hurt God continually, God continually seeks reconciliation... And even when we refuse to seek forgiveness God still loves us...

Jesus ends up with a little proverb: "What you bind on earth will be bound in heaven. What you loose on earth will be loosed in heaven."

No one knows for sure just what that is supposed to mean. But perhaps it means that relationships are forever. If we build them here – if we maintain them and heal their wounds and talk out problems and seek help – whether it's with our friends or husbands or wives or neighbors or children or parents – those relationships will go with us throughout eternity... but if we don't, we have lost a friend – forever. And friends just aren't all that easy to come by.

What Does Jesus Expect

Isaiah 5:1-7 and Matthew 21:33-43

The fruit of the Spirit is love, joy, peace, patience, kindness, goodness, faithfulness, gentleness and self-control.
Galatians 5:22

Listen to this – the last verse of our New Testament passage this morning – it's rather frightening... "I tell you that the Kingdom of God will be **taken away** from you and given to a people who will produce its fruit." That's the bottom line to the parable Jesus just told. You know the parable. You probably didn't even listen too closely when I read it a minute ago because it is so well known. In fact, I believe I used this very passage a year ago or so for a different sermon... A wealthy man builds a vineyard and a winepress as an investment. He leaves it in charge of some workers while he goes elsewhere. Later he sends others of his servants to collect the proceeds but the ones in charge of the vineyard have this strange idea that they have some claim to the proceeds, and even the business itself, so they kill the collectors. This doesn't happen just once but several times. Finally the businessman sends his son to do his bidding. He goes in confident that even the fools his father had hired wouldn't hurt the master's son. But wrong. They kill him too. What does the owner do? Well, of course he gets a posse together and goes in there and cleans out the wretches and starts over with new servants who will do the job and give him his due.

Jesus concludes – just in case we don't get the point – "I tell you that the kingdom of God – heaven itself – will be taken away from those who don't do the job and given to those who will."

So the big and important questions come up: "What exactly does God expect of us?" And "Have we met those expectations?" And of course, "What becomes of us if we fail?"

We can probably take great comfort in the fact that this parable isn't about us at all. Jesus is referring back to the passage in Isaiah that we used as our OT text this morning which describes God as being the vineyard and winepress owner and maker and Israel as the vineyard itself (as you can see, Jesus changed the imagery a bit, but the point is still the same). God had done all He possibly could to provide good soil and water for the grapes. He even searched until He found what He took to be the best grapes around. But when it came time to produce – nothing (for Jesus, it is bad servants that caused this – for Isaiah it is bad grapes – but either way, the result is the same). The producers, in either case, are the people of Israel. So technically that leaves us off the hook. In Isaiah God is going to wipe out the whole thing and start over. In Matthew, the owner is going to get rid of the old, unproductive servants and start over.

I think you could probably make some kind of anti-Semitism case here. But anyone who would do so has totally missed the point... That is that the new servants – the new grapes – are you and me. And, although both passages stop after the first "bad crop" is destroyed, the new crop – (of grapes or of servants) – will either produce or be liable for a more severe destruction.

I believe that Jesus is saying to his followers that the ball is now in our court and that, unless we DO something to produce the desired "fruit" (to mix a metaphor), we don't have a chance of entering the Kingdom of God. Eventually the owner will return and request to receive the increase. We had better produce.

The New Testament is full of this "fruit" idea. I suppose that is because the people of that day lived in a land where major crops were pomegranates, figs, grapes and other middle-eastern kinds of fruits. The people could relate to what Jesus was talking about. But we can understand it too. If the boss hires you to do a job and you don't do it, you get fired and someone else is hired. If he/she doesn't do the job either, they too, get fired...

So the questions: "What *does* God expect of us?" "Have we met those expectations?" "What does it mean if we are 'fired' ?"

Fortunately, fruit – not the kind you eat, but the kind you produce with your life – is described in the Bible in some detail. The best description of it is in Galatians 5 where it talks about the "fruit of the spirit". "The fruit of the Spirit", it says, "is love, joy, peace, patience, kindness, goodness, faithfulness, gentleness and self-control." Gal 5:22, 23 (NIV). **Those** are the things God expects us to be producing in our lives and in our world.

Galatians 5 is another of those passages we have heard a lot and think we know. But just how much of each of those things is really in *your* life and in *my* life? How much of each one is being shared with others and being built into others as a *result* of your own life? Let's think about each one for just a moment. I'll kind of direct the tour. You search through the reality of your life and determine how much fruit, if any, is really there...

LOVE – Ask yourself how much you really love others. Rate yourself on a scale of 1-100. Not just that special person in your life, but <u>everyone</u>. Put the beggar in the street, the different races and religions, the opposite political party, the old people, the young people, the handicapped, the person next to you this morning, the stranger, the person who doesn't agree with you, all into the same pot. Mix them up and ask, "How much do I love?" On a scale of 1-100...

Love needs to be one of the primary fruits you are producing.

JOY – When someone politely asks you "How are you?" what do you say inside? Do you have a sense of joy in just being alive? You may not really be feeling very well on any particular day. Maybe you have aches and pains. But God has given you *life.* The purpose of that life is to love and enjoy God.

There can be nothing but joy at the core of your being if you understand that and are part of God's family. What score do you give yourself on Joy?

PEACE – Do you ever feel guilty? Then your crop of peace is suffering. God gives forgiveness as we make confession of our sins. He gives a peace that is beyond anything else in this world.

You must be a person at peace – and you must be a peacemaker in all you do. How do you score with peace?

PATIENCE – I sometimes get impatient quickly. "Why doesn't that driver use his turn signal?" "Why can't she understand what I am trying to say?" "Why isn't everyone a little more like me? The world would sure be a better place."

It is US who need to learn to be more like Christ. To understand others and to be "patient" with them. God is working a continuing work in all of our lives. How much patience do you have – on a scale of 1-100?

KINDNESS AND GOODNESS – It's not very fashionable to be kind and good in our world today. Unless you claw and struggle and fight your way to the top – or wherever you are trying to get – you are thought of as setting yourself up for failure. But to God, *the kind person and the good person are successes in all they do.*

How kind are you, really? How good?

FAITHFULNESS – I don't know whether this is a religious "faithfulness" or not. I don't think so. I think it has more to do with something we, today, might call LOYALTY. I believe most of us are sorely lacking in it. Ask yourself: Do you "faithfully" attend church? What things might keep you from it? Are these things really more important? Would you *gladly* turn off Monday night football or the good programs on TV on Thursday nights to talk to a friend in need? Have you ever spoken in a disparaging way about your spouse or your children or your church leaders or your minister? Do you pray for the president of the U.S. and other political leaders? Or do you pray regularly at all?

To *WHAT and to WHOM you are loyal says a great deal about who you are as an individual. HOW loyal you are says a great deal about your character.* How do you score?

GENTLENESS AND SELF-CONTROL – I've lumped these two together because I think they are so closely related. A person who is self-controlled is almost always a gentleman or a gentlewoman. When you and I go out there and relate to others, we ought to be viewed as a person of class – a person of gentleness – a person who is able to keep his or her emotions and reactions in check. Again, this isn't one of those things that is greatly valued in our society. You may be viewed as weak or as a wimp. In fact, it may even be costly. You may not always make the sale. You may not always get what you want. You may have to be just a bit smarter in order not to get taken advantage of. But you will produce good fruit. Those who see you will know that it is the God within you that allows you to have dignity and not "lose it" as is most common.

Jesus is our example of this. No one was ever more gentle or self-controlled. Yet no one influenced the lives of those He touched more than He did.

How gentle are you? How much self-control do you exercise?

"I tell you that the Kingdom of God will be **taken away** from you and given to a people who will produce its fruit [if you and I do not]."

YOU'VE GOT TO HAVE A DREAM

Isaiah 43:16-21 and Philippians 3:7-14

Forget the former things; do not dwell on the past. See, I am doing a new thing! Now it springs up; do you not perceive it? I am making a way in the desert and streams in the wasteland.
Isaiah 43:18, 19

There are very few professions that I can think of, where ones' husband or wife gets the chance to observe what you do on a regular basis unless he or she is employed at the same place. The ministry, of course, is one. Typically, after church – on Sunday afternoon, I have the opportunity to hear just what a totally unbiased and straightforwardly honest congregation member has to say about the sermon or the worship service or anything else that goes on Sunday mornings.

Last Sunday Sue didn't say much right after church. That usually is a good sign so I like to leave it at that. But shortly after we got home she asked me whether I had read a certain article in the newspaper. I hadn't. But that was OK because she had already torn it out for me to read. She handed it to me and said, "Read it." "It will make a good sermon." "Do it soon."

I dutifully took the article and put it with some things I would be bringing over to the church later. On Wednesday I finally got around to reading it. As usual, she had given good advice. It was very worthwhile. It was an article titled "Field of Vision." It wasn't about eyesight, but about what it called the "buzzword" for the 90's. It was about forward looking "vision" – insight into the future to see what *can be* and *how* it may come about and, of course, people who have it (vision).

I was just a little concerned when the author called "vision" the "hot word" of this generation – like "synergistic" and "guru" were the "hot words" of the 70's and 80's. I have always been a strong believer in "vision". I've always wished (and at the same time not wished) that *I* were a visionary... that *I* could see what is and ask "why" and see what could be and ask "why not?"

"Vision," to me, is a very Christian concept. The Old and New Testament are both filled with it. In fact, one passage in the Old Testament even suggests, "Where there is no vision, the people perish." Paul talks about pressing onward toward the goal – and he "sees" what the prize is at the end...

The whole idea of "vision" is a very comforting concept to most of us. Those who believe in vision and visionaries have hope. They can take comfort in the fact that they believe that *someone* can see into the future as it ought to be and figure out how to get us there. It's especially comforting when society and the economy are in uncertain times. A person likes to believe that, even if no one seems to know the answers, there IS someone out there that will come forward and save the day. Unfortunately, there is a tremendous shortage of visionaries in reality. VERY FEW people can see so clearly what ought to be that it takes on substance.

But vision does, on occasion, happen. John Hoyle, a professor at Texas A&M says, "Vision is a step beyond creativity... There are a lot of creative people who do not have the ability to grasp the big picture. There's a real gift, a charismatic aura about visionaries... Not everybody has it. It's a lot like beauty. It's difficult to find [or to define]. But you know it when you see it."

Today, being "Reformation Sunday," is the perfect time to be thinking about visionaries. Martin Luther most certainly was one. He looked at the church and saw how entangled it had become with its traditions and dogma and saw what it *ought* to be like. Then he boldly stepped out and nailed his thesis to the church door and the world has never been the same since.

Or perhaps you've heard of a man named Millard Fuller. He was a lawyer in Georgia who you might call a visionary. He had a great job and abundant talent that made him a millionaire by the time he was 29. That was his vision for himself. That is what he set out to accomplish and he did. He thought he had the world by the tail. Then, one day, he went home to find that his wife had left him. She drove a Lincoln Continental and had a household staff – everything a wife could want – except she had no husband – and she wanted one... So she left – went out to find another life that was better than the one she had...

At that point Millard Fuller was forced to re-evaluate his life and worked to set some priorities and to establish a new vision. He managed to reconcile with his wife – he promised to change his ways – and, together, they established a new vision that involved *both* of their lives.

They decided they needed to give away all of their money and the things money can buy and be wholly committed to their vision. The vision – to put people into clean, well-built homes. They called their new effort, "Habitat for Humanity". And today "Habitat for Humanity" is throughout the world (including Detroit), using volunteers to rehabilitate old houses for low-income families.

Fuller and his wife say that their new vision – and all real vision must be this way – was to look at things from God's viewpoint, instead of an egocentric viewpoint. "[Having vision]," they say, "is rising above your own narrow self-interests, not just looking out for *your* husband, *your* wife, *your own* children. Not just loving those who are like you." Real vision is something God does IN a person.

500 years ago, Martin Luther had a vision. Things could be much better than they were. He saw the church getting rid of 1500 years worth of accumulated baggage and accomplishing something wonderful and new for Christ. 104 years ago a handful of people on Mt. Hope Ave. in Detroit had a vision. They too, "saw" what could be. They didn't have visions of grandeur. They simply saw a church where people could come together and love one another without debating all kinds of peripheral theologies and doctrines. They saw a place where Jesus was honored in the highest sense of the word – **through the lives of the people.**

I wonder what our vision is today? In a general sense of the term, every Christian IS a visionary. If we read the Bible we learn very quickly what the world is *supposed* to look like and what it *will* look like when Jesus comes back. Throughout the Bible we see that evil will be punished and the good will be raised up. We read that whoever is a follower of the Lord Jesus will inherit the eternal kingdom and whoever is opposed to the righteousness and the righteous of God will not. We read of a "new heaven and a new earth." We read of the destruction of the world as we know it and a kingdom of peace where God will rule. And this sort of "vision" goes on and on...

But in a more personal sense, what is YOUR vision and MY vision? I'm not talking about the vision we have as a CHURCH. OUR vision is hopefully very similar to the vision of our founding fathers and mothers... to have a church family that loves one another and worships Christ in harmony and peace... to have a faith that, as a body, ministers to the community and to the world. As a church, our vision is to draw others into the faith through what we demonstrate in our lives. And of course, if we don't, we fail ourselves and our vision is invalid.

What is YOUR vision? Every one of us knows people who have been deeply influenced by the life of another; whose life wouldn't have the quality or the beauty it does if it hadn't been for someone caring. The vision for you and me, perhaps, needs to be in the "seeing" of what Christ can do through us on a daily, regular basis.

The index card in today's bulletin is a recognition of someone's vision. Someone, in YOUR life, has been important. Maybe that wasn't by design nor intention, but it came because someone was acting out what it means to live as a Christian in their world. THAT is the greatest vision any of us can capture. What is my life like? Why am I like that? How COULD it or SHOULD it be? Why can't it be!?

If you are a Christian, your vision is constantly to live life more daily like Jesus... to walk your daily walk more like his... to talk every word you speak more like his... to set your mind on things positive and good and helpful and loving *always* like his.

There isn't, perhaps, any greater expression of this that I know of, than the hymn we sang earlier, "Be Thou My Vision." Turn to that, if you would, and let's look at the words (sometimes singing makes us skip over the words so quickly that we don't listen). Number 382. It's a prayer. Let's read it in unison as a prayer...

> *Be Thou my Vision, O Lord of my heart;*
> *Naught be all else to me, save that Thou art.*
> *Thou my best Thought, by day or by night,*
> *Waking or sleeping, Thy presence my light.*
>
> *Be Thou my Wisdom, and Thou my true Word;*
> *I ever with Thee and Thou with me, Lord;*
> *Thou my great Father, I Thy true son;*
> *Thou in me dwelling, and I with Thee one.*
>
> *Be Thou my battle Shield, Sword for the fight;*
> *Be Thou my Dignity, Thou my Delight;*
> *Thou my soul's Shelter, Thou my high Tower:*
> *Raise Thou me heavenward, O Power of my power.*
>
> *Riches I heed not, nor man's empty praise,*
> *Thou mine Inheritance, now and always:*

Thou and Thou only, first in my heart,
High King of Heaven, my Treasure Thou art.

High King of Heaven, my victory won,
May I reach Heaven's joys, O bright Heaven's Sun!
Heart of my own heart, whatever befall,
Still be my Vision, O Ruler of all.

                                                    Amen.

THE DREAMER

Acts 10:9-16 and Genesis 37.

He saw heaven opened and something like a large sheet being let down to earth by its four corners.... This happened three times, and immediately the sheet was taken back to heaven.
Acts 10:11, 16

There are some wonderful characters portrayed in the Bible. I think that one of my very favorite is Joseph – not the Joseph of "Mary and Joseph," the human parents of Jesus – but Joseph, youngest son of Jacob – the one with the coat of many colors. The one who had dreams and saw himself, because of those dreams, ruling over his brothers. The one who didn't have enough sense to keep some of his dreams to himself and incurred the jealousy and hatred of his half-brothers, who ultimately sold him into slavery... Joseph, the genius who insured the continuation of God's people during a world-wide famine. Joseph, who doing his best, ended up having the nation of Israel become captives of Egypt for 400 years.

Joseph was always a dreamer, but when he was a young fellow of 17 God gave him a dream that changed his life and would go on to change the world. It was a dream that held great potential for a successful life for himself but also wonderful blessings and prosperity for others – and a pathway for saving his own family from starvation.

The reason Joseph's dream was so effective is that it came from God and Joseph never doubted that. It was a dream that identified Joseph with the God of the universe as opposed to the typical kind of human dreams which link us with people or events or things...

Most of the dreams in our own lives are rather short lived or subject to massive revision. When we reach the age of about 40 we take another look at some of the dreams of our youth and conclude that they aren't going to become reality unless something happens **NOW**... It becomes time to **redirect – rededicate – reinforce** those dreams. I'm not talking about "mid-life crisis", but rather something that is at the very core of ones being... A dream that really does come from God. Maybe your dream has never been verbalized but it's a dream about how you want to become or be... what you desire to "look like" in relation to God... It's a dream about the big issues of personal life and friendship and leadership and righteousness... It is a dream that is based on faith. The Bible talks about faith being the "substance of things hoped for." That "hope" is our dream. It doesn't even exist aside from faith.

I wonder what your dream is today. What do you want God to see when He looks at you? Which direction do you see yourself going in terms of righteousness? Is your faith growing or shrinking? Is your "goodness" and "love" going deeper or is it evaporating? What **is** the content of that terribly personal and private dream of your life?

Most dreams cost something if they are to become reality. That, of course, is the reason most of our dreams never do. Joseph spent *13 years* in prison and in servitude to pay for the dream. But that was the cost of seeing the dream fulfilled. If you want to accomplish anything worthwhile in life, you must go beyond your daily routine, doing much more than the minimum required. You must step out and take some risks.

Joseph took a big risk. He publicly stated his dream. That is usually not too wise. His brothers are already aware that their father loves Joseph more than any of them because he is the baby of the family and the son of his favorite wife, Rachel. One day Joseph finds them all together and says, "Hey, guys, listen to my dream... I dreamed that we were all out in the field doing the harvest, shocking the grain and getting it ready for the threshers to come. All of a sudden my sheaf stands up straight and tall and all of yours start coming toward mine and gathered around and bowed down to it..." "Pretty wild, huh?"

Pretty wild indeed. It doesn't take a genius to know what that dream is about. They didn't like the implications one bit...

Joseph has another dream, somewhat like the first. He decides to share it too. This time he sees himself at the very center of the universe and the sun and the moon and eleven stars bow down to him.

Even his father is troubled by this one. "You mean you believe that not only your brothers will one day bow down to you but that your mother and I will too?"

How wise his sharing of his dreams was is uncertain, but ultimately the bowing down is exactly what happened – brothers and parents alike – in Egypt, many years later.

The dreamer is sent on a mission to see how his brothers, shepherds by vocation, are doing. They see him coming with his fancy coat on and decide that this is a great opportunity to do away with him. "... then we'll see what becomes of his dreams... "

But a dream that is put in place by God is not so easily thwarted. What Joseph or you or I are destined to do or become, if we are faithful and always moving toward it, will happen. This is an important point... God has something for you or me to do or become. If we are willing to follow what God has for us, it WILL come to pass. The brothers decided to kill Joseph and throw him into a cistern and tell their father that a wild animal got him. Reuben, the second youngest, suggested that maybe killing him wasn't a good idea. We should just throw him into the cistern and let him die there (he planned to go later and rescue him). We can still take his coat and bloody it and tell father that he was killed.

But, of course, Joseph is pulled out of the cistern and sold to some passing caravan as a slave – and this makes the dream, even though it seems even more impossible now, possible.

Sometimes I think God enjoys doing what seems to be impossible. The scene is set here for Joseph and his brothers to NEVER see one another again. In fact, that was the intention of the brothers. They DID take his coat and soak it in blood and take it to their father, telling him his youngest and most beloved son had been torn to pieces by wild animals. The dream most certainly had come to an end.

But meanwhile, the caravan of Midianites re-sold Joseph to a man named Potiphar, one of the Pharaoh's officials – a captain of the guard – setting the stage for some real possibilities.

In our own lives, God is constantly doing the same kind of thing. WE know what the dream is. Most of us haven't shared it with anyone. It's a secret in our own hearts. It's our deepest ambition and the thing that would make our lives worth living if it could ever come to pass... It has nothing to do with material goals, most likely. It has only to do with that part of us that has been made in the image of God himself. Often our very lives and the situations in which we find ourselves make the dream seem impossible. *"God can never use me in that way." "Too much has happened to make it possible." "I'm a prisoner to my current situation. I can't change." "My life is near it's end. I've done all I can do."*

I tell you, God loves to take those very thoughts and prove us wrong. If we have courage to move ahead for God... if we have courage to face realities and know that God can overcome situations and circumstances... if we have courage to admit that we need to have God's assistance... if we have the courage to welcome some changes into our lives, God will use us in marvelous and wonderful ways.

Each of our lives has a wonderful potential – no matter how old or young we are. We can do something significant for God and for our world if we are committed to following Him... to stepping out and taking some risks and being patient.

Be a dreamer for God. Never let it go. It's about you and what you are here for. God will help as we are willing to be committed to listening to Him and to righteousness and to action.

IS MATTER ALL THAT MATTERS?

Ecclesiastes 6:1-6 and Mark 10:17-31

Jesus looked at him and loved him. "One thing you lack," he said. "Go, sell everything you have and give to the poor, and you will have treasure in heaven. Then come, follow me." At this the man's face fell. He went away sad, because he had great wealth. Jesus looked around and said to his disciples, "How hard it is for the rich to enter the kingdom of God!"

Mark 10:21-23

When I was growing up I never heard of Lent. Most of you probably had the same experience. "Lent" was too tied to Catholicism to be observed in the Protestant church. If you ask many Protestants even today what Lent is they will be hard pressed to define it.

The most obvious element of Lent, for most people, is the "giving up" of something for a period of time. For the more religiously attuned, Lent is that period of time where we begin to think about Jesus' crucifixion and resurrection in a more concentrated way and is, perhaps, even a time of self-examination. But very few, I would guess, can put it all together and tell you what the "giving up" part of Lent has to do with paying attention to the cross and the resurrection and to our own spiritual lives... Some may postulate that the self-denial has to do with identifying with Jesus as he denied himself and suffered on the cross for our sins. Not a bad guess, but if you think about it, giving up chocolate or TV for 40 days or not eating red meat or fast food or things like that that most people do to commemorate Lent, it is almost ludicrous compared with the suffering and humiliation and death of the cross.

You might even think of the "giving up" as a penance. You sin and this is the way you work it out to make it right with God. But that idea rejects the very work of Jesus on the cross. What he did there is to become the sacrifice that completely pays for our sins. There isn't <u>anything</u> we can do more than has already been done. Our sins have been completely paid for. They are no more. There is no longer anything to pay for. Jesus died as full payment.

If you have always thought that Lenten sacrifice – giving up something you enjoy for a season – is a form of "fast" you come pretty close. In the Old Testament times and in Jesus day, the "fast" was a method of mourning. The idea was that you were <u>so</u> grief stricken that you could not eat – you didn't care to eat – food meant nothing to you whatsoever...

I guess, for me, it would be more meaningful to give up food entirely for a 24-hour period once in a while and "feel" the hunger that would remind me how much grief hurts and how hard it is to bear.

Self-denial, penance, fasting. These are usually what we think of when we seriously consider what Lent is about. But I think the significance of "giving up" something goes much deeper. It is a concrete recognition that that part of us which is spiritual has a direct connection to that part of our lives that is material. Our society bombards us with the notion that **we are what we own.** Our identity is tied up in the things we possess. We feel better about ourselves, we are told, if we own more. If we buy the right car, own a home in the right neighborhood, buy designer clothes, use the right toothpaste... One study estimated that by the time teen-agers graduate from high-school they will have watched 350,000 TV commercials. ... All telling them that the "good life" can be had in materialism.

Gail Sheehy, in her book, *Pathfinders*, gives the results of a survey. She says, "When two thousand young men were asked to spell out their greatest concerns for the future, they expressed two major fears in equal weight – and absolute contradiction; fear of not having enough money, and fear of being locked in by the constant pursuit of money." [1]

Stacey Woods, the founder of the Inter-Varsity Christian Fellowship in the United States wrote, "A Christian must realize that material possessions have no permanent value. Supply and demand, the rise and fall of the stock market, changes in taste and fashion, the movement of society and the inevitable process of decay and obsolescence make much of what we have of temporary value... How easily we citizens of heaven, secure in Christ Jesus find our imagined security in earthly things!"[2]

Friday evening Sue and I and Rachel went to see "Shindler's List". It is a movie about the holocaust. I recommend it highly. I think it ought to be required viewing for every person of righteousness. The single most significant scene in the movie, for me, was when all was over one of the characters, in bitter tears, confessed that perhaps if he had sold his car or given up his brotherhood pin, one more life could have been saved. The car, the pin, the money – **nothing** means anything really. The material world is only temporary but it sucks us in and blinds us until we can't see what is really important...

You see, the things we own tend to blind us to the spiritual aspects of reality. Materialism is dangerous because it destroys the spiritual roots of our lives.

As much as I wouldn't want you to go out and buy her record, the singer Madonna, in her song "Material World" illustrates quite well the impact of materialism. The people singing the refrain in the background sound like monotonous robots – machines with no soul. Materialism – love of the things we own, and lust for the things we don't yet own, obscures our grasp of reality. It actually destroys the capacity for spiritual faith... Or, if not actually destroying it, it certainly blunts it significantly. Our knowledge of God – our love for God – becomes empty. If we can't see it, touch it, taste it, smell it or measure it, we doubt that it's real...

It's really hard for spiritual riches to compete with material ones. On a daily basis, I must admit, I am usually more preoccupied with working to put money in the bank than I am with following Jesus' admonition to store up treasure in heaven... and I have a job that keeps spiritual thing ever before me. What must it be like for all of you?

In the book of Revelations, Jesus rebukes the church at Laodicea for its material affluence and its spiritual ignorance. He said, "You say, 'I am rich; I have acquired wealth and do not need a thing.' But you do not realize that you are wretched, pitiful, poor, blind and naked." (Rev. 3:17). I wonder if that is us...

So what do we do about it? How can we maintain spiritual wealth in a material world? Well, one idea that some have proposed is to determine how much is enough in our lives. Just how much money do I and my family really <u>need</u>? What will make us comfortable and pay the bills? What kind of a house is enough for us to take pride in without being so much that we can become prideful? Let's determine those levels and give the rest away. I've always liked that idea. We all tend to live to the extent of our income – maybe just a bit beyond. But really, most of us have far more than we need. Our full basements and annual rummage sales prove it.

Some of the monastic orders (maybe all of them, I'm not sure) take vows of poverty. They don't do that just because its fun. They do it because they realize that the material world – possessions of all kinds – often stand in the way of spirituality.

But God is the creator of heaven AND earth. Jesus is Lord over the spiritual AND the physical – the visible AND the invisible. It is our job to live in the tension between the two... Not becoming monastic in our faith – nor greedy in our ownership. That's the fine line we are called to walk.

I think there is only one way to walk that fine line. That is to spend some time on a regular basis in meditation... I'm not talking about some Eastern religion sort of thing where you enter some kind of trance. I'm talking about simply taking some time to spend with God every day. J.I. Packer describes meditation as "an activity of holy thought, consciously performed in the presence of God, under the eye of God, by the help of God, as a means of communication with God. Its purpose is to clear one's mental and spiritual vision of God and let his truth make its full and proper impact on one's mind and heart."[3]

What this means is, that you and I can keep our perspective on materialism and spirituality **by simply pausing each day to focus on God**. It might be while driving to work or instead of reading the paper so thoroughly in the morning or in place of the TODAY show. It might be in the evening just before dropping off to sleep. But in each of our days, at some point, we need to spend time talking to God about the cares of our lives and acknowledging just who God is and His greatness... Not always thinking about what WE are about, but considering WHO is with us.

Lent is a season of spiritual reflection. Whether you "give up" something or not is not really terribly important unless it speaks to you of the place of material things in your life... unless it draws you closer to the God who loves you and sacrificed all that we might live forever. We live in a material world, but we are NOT wholly material people.

---

[1] *Pathfinders*, Gail Sheehy, p. 55
[2] *Some Ways of God*, C. Stacey Woods, p. 86
[3] *Knowing God*, J.I.Packer, p. 19

INTENTIONAL FRIENDS.

Proverbs 27:17 and I Corinthians 12:1-11

As iron sharpens iron, so one man sharpens another.
Proverbs 27:17

I tend to be an "idea" person. You have probably gathered that over the years. My ideas aren't always very good and sometimes I try to implement the ideas before they are well thought out but, over the years, we've done some fun things together. Remember "God's Money"? Writing our own centennial hymn? Remember the newspaper ad campaign with the cartoons? If you are around long enough you too, will have the opportunity to sigh and ask "What's Steve up to now?"

Several years ago I came up with the idea that we could pay for mailings to new Livonia residents by putting a little card into the mailing with a magnet on the back. The card would contain emergency numbers for fire and police and also some community businesses that might be useful to new people in town. The businesses would pay to have their businesses listed. We did that for a year and it worked pretty well but was a lot of work to get the "sponsors" and became a lot easier just to pay for the mailings ourselves.

One of the sponsors was a Christian counseling service. The owner wasn't content simply to send his money and be listed. He wanted to meet me. We made an appointment to go to lunch together. I liked Jeff well enough, I guess, but was really rather nervous around him. The guy was a psychologist so tended to analyze everything. I must admit that I've never come across anyone who could make me talk so much. When I talked he listened and responded and asked questions... He made me feel pretty important (if you ever feel the need to see a counselor – do. It's amazing what a trained person can bring out in the open – and a specifically "Christian" one can help you see things in the proper perspective) But I knew what he was doing – he was analyzing me... I didn't want to be analyzed nor did I really like it very much after a while...

Jeff was young – my age – he owned his own business – had people working for him – had plenty of clients – loved his church – but I don't think he had many friends. In me I think he saw someone who he didn't have to counsel, he didn't have to supervise, he didn't have to be a deacon with... He saw a potential friend.

We had lunch together just about every month for a couple of years. I usually dreaded our times together and often resented them. He was just too intense for me... always analyzing everything... always asking why and probing and seeking and exploring, but never really "giving" much of himself – he found it almost impossible to separate himself from his work and to <u>stop</u> being a listener... I pointed that out to him one day and he immediately tried to analyze his own personality and why I would say such a thing... Eventually he turned his counseling service over to others and went off, himself, to work on a Ph.D. out of state... I haven't seen nor heard from him since...

During our times together, Jeff and I knocked some of the rough edges off one another. I began to think about things I said and did a little more analytically. He found out that it is possible that people might just like him even if he isn't always "Mr. Counselor."

A verse from Proverbs: (27:17) "As iron sharpens iron, so a man sharpens his friend."

Friends smooth our rough edges and make us as useful in our world and to our God as we possibly can be... Some friendships come easily and are strong and there is never any kind of tension or friction. Those are a great blessing. If they are able to withstand some of the hardships of life that come our way and that friend sticks with you and supports you and loves you through it all, you have found a treasure... But some friendships take some conscious effort to maintain... and most of us won't do that. If a friend demands too much, we allow ourselves to drift apart

Too often we fall into relationships because they are convenient and too seldom because they are challenging or ordered by God. Too seldom do we enter into relationships with a higher view in mind – a view toward doing Gods work in that persons life and allowing that person to do God's work of sharpening and smoothing and shaping in our own.

Sue and I had been married three years when we moved to Massachusetts to attend seminary. We knew no one on the entire east coast. It was rather frightening... so far away from home – no friends – no family – no idea even where we were going to live. We met a couple of other students on our first day in the seminary cafeteria but none of them seemed to be strong potential friends... We found a tiny apartment on the third floor of a 200 year old house which had been converted into an office building in Salem (we were sort of the resident security guards). One evening, while we were questioning God as to why He brought us to such a low point in our lives we heard something strange at our windows. We looked out and down below was one of the couples we had met, tossing stones up at our windows to get our attention (the building had no door bell and it was locked up tight for the night). They wanted to be friends... and they became good ones over the course of the next three years... and thus far over the past 2 decades.

Friendship, sometimes, ought to be an *"intentional* activity". Sometimes it ought to be entered into with the idea of giving part of yourself to another person – and with the full knowledge that in so doing, you will get even more in return.

You met my friend Ralph back in February when he preached here. He and I were roommates in college and I've always thought of our relationship as like that between Jonathan and David in the Bible who we looked at a few weeks ago. During our senior year we decided NOT to room together. We chose roommates who were a couple of years younger than ourselves from among our Inter Varsity Christian Fellowship group. We knew they were young in their faith and we wanted to nurture them and help them grow... We sacrificed our "easy" friendship for a time for the sake of befriending a couple of fellows who needed friends. I'd like to report that those two fellows responded wonderfully well to our sacrifice and became spiritual giants and are missionaries proclaiming the gospel to people in some foreign land now – but I can't. It was a miserable year and we were all glad when it ended. But Ralph and I grew perhaps more in OUR faith in that year than in any other of our lives. ... And I like to think that those two fellows look back on the year and would say they experienced a little of Christ's love through us...

Several people have approached me in the weeks before FRIEND DAY and told me that they have no friends who are not already involved in churches – they had no one to invite as a friend... That was very troubling to me... When the Christian community becomes so ingrown that it is not in regular relationship with those outside of the fellowship of faith, the church cannot survive... When we have ceased to make friends with those who need Christian friends and a Christian influence in their lives, we have neglected to be faithful to the great commission of Christ – to go into all the world and make disciples... You can't make disciples if you always hang around with disciples...

What would have happened if Jesus had not eaten with publicans and sinners? What would have happened if the disciples had stayed in that upper room after Jesus' resurrection? What would have happened if the New Testament church would have failed to bring their friends and relatives into the fellowship or if Paul had decided it was better to stay at home than to risk his life and reputation traveling throughout the world associating with all sorts of people?... What will happen if Christians today know only other Christians?

It is up to us to actively seek friends outside of the church... not to convert them or "use" them as token "pagans" but because Christ directed us to by his word and by his example and because "As iron sharpens iron, so a man sharpens his friends." ... We will be better people because of it – and so will they.

There are people out there who *need* you as a friend. They may be much different than you but sometimes that is the relationship to which God calls you... And I believe that you already know the person God wants you to be friends with. Dave Miller said he couldn't think of a friend to invite for FRIEND DAY last week until that prayer for friends we had the week before when we bowed our heads and asked God to bring someone to mind. He said it was like a vision – immediately he knew who he ought to invite... You don't have to go out into the streets of Detroit and pick up some hopeless derelict – <u>someone</u> in your neighborhood or in you place of employment or the place you "hang out" for fun needs you as a friend. God has assigned you to them and unless you show them the love of Christ, they may never know it.

Friendship has no age barriers. One of my closest friends is nearly my fathers age – I've seen people in their 70's and 80's make friends with children, teenagers make friends with first graders. You know, the friend God has assigned to you may be in this room right now... If you are an older person, it may be a child or one of our teens who need to have a "grandparent" take an interest in them... If you are a young couple, maybe God wants you to reach out to a senior whose family is less than attentive... Maybe God wants YOU to be an **intentional** friend. Don't be narrow in your perspective of who can be your friend – *anyone* can be.

When I graduated from college, a group of my friends gave me a Bible – they all signed it and someone wrote a quote from Bruce Larson in the back. It says, "To love is to trust, and to trust is to reveal those things about yourself that could give someone else the weapons with which to hurt you. Until we can be this vulnerable we cannot truly love. And it is not enough to be vulnerable to God; we must also be vulnerable to our friends."

Jesus said, "I no longer call you servants, but friends" then he gave his life – intentionally – and died for you and for me. Friends, He is to be our model. Let us give our lives – intentionally – to others – let us make our world "friends" of Jesus.

SAND CASTLES

Ezekiel 33:30-33; John 6:27-29.

To them you are nothing more than one who sings love songs with a beautiful voice and plays an instrument well, for they hear your words but do not put them into practice.
Ezekiel 33:32

When I was young I used to sit through sermons every Sunday that lasted at least an hour. I can't say I remember even one of them (although I must admit that I don't remember my own sermons after a couple of days either). But as my mind wondered I would often think about Jesus (so maybe the sermons weren't so bad after all). I though about some of the things he said and the ways he said them. I concluded he must have been a <u>very</u> interesting guy and I wished I could have heard him...

Jesus was always telling stories. If he wanted to make a point, he told a story. If he wanted to get out of a tight spot, he told a story. If he wanted to preach a sermon, he told a story. I wondered, if Jesus is our example, why ministers didn't just tell stories instead of getting into all that boring theology and lecturing and putting us all to sleep...

I didn't realize at the time that I would be in that spot myself one day. But now I know why. Jesus taught in parables because that is where people are at. We all love a good story. We remember stories for a long time. Often we will even repeat the story to someone else and embellish it a bit... or even tell it just as we heard it... Ministers don't preach in stories because it is simply too hard to do. Story telling demands a great deal of creativity. It demands a certain ability to tell... Usually stories are short and don't fill up enough time so that the people in the congregation won't feel they've gotten their money's worth... And, finally, but maybe most significant – the best stories are almost all fiction – they aren't true

– and it is always embarrassing when someone comes up after the service and says, "That was a great story. I can't believe you... Did you really do that?"... Ministers just have a hard time coming out and saying, "No. That was a lie." And you wouldn't want them to say that anyway, would you?

So, treading on rather shaky ground, I'm hoping this year to do a "story sermon" about once each month... But you mustn't ever ask me if they are true. They most likely are <u>based</u> on some thread of truth or some perception of truth in my convoluted mind, but the point is the <u>point</u> the story makes – not the story itself...

Jesus said, [Mat 7:24-27] *[Listen], "everyone who hears these words of mine and puts them into practice is like a wise man who built his house on the rock. The rain came down, the streams rose, and the winds blew and beat against that house; yet it did not fall, because it had its foundation on the rock. But everyone who hears these words of mine and does not put them into practice is like a foolish man who built his house on sand. The rain came down, the streams rose, and the winds blew and beat against that house, and it fell with a great crash."*

When I was a boy, my parents took us for some kind of vacation every summer. Sometimes it was to the mountains. Sometimes it was to some fun kind of place. Sometimes it seemed as though we had no destination at all – we drove for two weeks stopping here and there to see interesting things – I suppose my parents knew where we were heading, but we seldom did... But on at least 2 summers, we went to a lake with a sandy shore to relax and swim and ski and do whatever we wanted...

One summer I met a friend named Dave. Dave and I became fast friends and we began to scheme and plan and dream. We took on the challenge that has faced young boys confronted with acres of sandy beach for centuries. We decided to build a castle – the biggest and best sand castle anyone had ever seen or even thought of. We laid it out on the beach and thought through each section... Then we began to build...

We firmly packed the sand, mixing the driest of the sand with water to form a foundation that would not crumble. It seemed to us as solid as concrete (but, of course, it wasn't). Then we began construction of the great wall, a huge structure more than a foot thick. It went all around the perimeter of the castle compound. It was a great wall, reinforced with mud and stones and plant stems we had gathered from the water's edge. When you build a castle, the wall is the most important. You have to keep out the myriad of invaders who might come along to wage war...

Inside the wall was the fanciest layout you could find. We arranged rooms this way and that and created scores of windows overlooking the countryside. There were huge doors on the front of the castle and secret entrances and tunnels running throughout...

In the very center of the complex we built the most magnificent tower you can imagine... Every castle has to have a great tower. Where else could you keep prisoners and keep a watch for enemies approaching miles away...

Finally, we built a mote around the whole thing. It was wide enough that no one would even dare to think about trying to cross. It was infested with crocodiles. It's banks were like sheer cliffs...

When you're young, you have a strange perspective on history, so right next to our tenth century tower was a huge garage for our Cadillac's and Rolls Royce's... In another part of the castle was a wonderful heated swimming pool with a water slide, and on one section of the great wall, there was a smoothed off area to be used as a landing strip... It didn't matter. This was our dream and minor inconsistencies didn't bother us...

It took us most of the afternoons and mornings of two days to build the castle. Everyone said it was marvelous. When it was all finished we stood back with pride and admired our creation – then grabbed our towels and went swimming.

A few hours later, however something terrible happened. Suddenly clouds started rolling in and the wind began to blow and the sky became dark. The waves churned and the rain began falling in torrents... NOTHING could stop the wind and the water. Our majestic castle began to crumble. The moat melted away. We piled our trucks and cars and shovels in the path of the water, but they were too little too late... The water rushed in from every side, ripping our castle to pieces... Within minutes there was nothing left – no recognizable buildings, no wall, no moat – just the memory. We fought back tears and promised to re-build it – but we never did... It was gone.

Jesus is saying in his story that sometimes violent storms appear in real life and not only in the play-world of children. Unless our foundations are built on solid ground – on rock that will not crumble – our hopes and futures might wash away as quickly as the castle made of sand. ANYONE who builds his/her life on the transitory and shifting sand will eventually slide into the sea... It's not a question as to whether this will happen – it's a question of "when."

Storms will certainly come to each of us; winds will blow fiercely against our lives. But if we build our lives on a solid foundation – if we center our focus and values on the rock, then we can never be destroyed.

In this parable, Jesus defines two very distinct lifestyles – one positive, the other negative. The implication is that, although we have a choice in the matter, one of the choices is foolish and one is wise.

My sister and I always loved to play hide-and-seek. It didn't really matter much whether other kids were around to join in. If so, that was great, but if it was just the two of us, that was fine too... But we had very different philosophies of the game. Kathy would take the 30-40 seconds of my hiding my eyes to find the perfect hiding place. Once there, she would barely breath, make no sound whatsoever and she was nearly impossible to find. Sometimes, after I'd gotten tired of searching, I'd go get my mother to call her to come out of hiding – the game was over – she had won... And sometimes she still stayed hidden.

But when **I** hid, it was a different story. I wanted, above everything else to be found. It seemed a terrible waste of time to sit there in silence waiting to be discovered. I would clear my throat loudly, I would rustle leaves, I would even trying to run from one hiding place to another – a sure way of being discovered...

Jesus talks about rocks and sand – wise and foolish – playing life by the rules God established or doing it on our own. We just don't have enough experience in life to attempt to do it on our own.

There was once a wealthy developer who had made his fortune designing and constructing single-family homes in a fast-growing suburb. He had built thousands and made millions of dollars – high quality, reasonably priced homes...

One of his best employees was a construction superintendent who had been involved in the building of the majority of these homes... He had spent most of his working life working faithfully for this man. He hoped to retire soon.

The developer himself was getting a bit older and was spending more and more of his time in Florida during the winter months... One year, during late fall, he decided to go south for the longest stay yet, so he called in his trusted building specialist to give him instructions. He said to him: "Joe, you've been with me many years and I totally trust you and appreciate the fact that I can leave and put you in charge and not worry about anything. While I am gone this winter, I want you to build a very special home for me. I want it to be the finest you have ever constructed. Use the best materials, hire the best crews. Be very careful –

the quality is far more important than the cost. Spend whatever you have to – you have a blank check. When I come back, I expect to see the finest home you have ever built."

The superintendent went to work immediately, but as he became involved in the project, it suddenly occurred to him that he could make a great deal of money for his retirement if he used inferior construction materials. He could use them below the surface where no one could see them. He could get away with it. The house would be sub-standard, but probably no one would ever know...

He ordered marginal lumber. He used 2X4's where he should have used 2X6's. Where he should have used good, solid 3/4 inch plywood, he used half inch. Where he should have used high-grade insulation, he used cheaper insulation. Where he should have used the best plumbing materials, he cut more corners... The house looked sensational from the outside, but the infrastructure was not very good at all.

In the spring, when the developer returned, he drove out right away to look at this dream house. He expected something extraordinary, and he wasn't disappointed. As far as he could tell this was truly a great house in every way.

The developer was overcome with gratitude to his long time friend and trusted employee. He said, "In gratefulness for your many years of service, I want to give you the keys to this new home. It's yours! You , of all people, deserve it."

Each of us are entrusted to build our lives in the best way we possibly can for God. We are told to build on a firm foundation of kindness and respect – to develop in our lives the words spelled out here on this beautiful banner [fruit of the spirit]. But occasionally we are tempted to throw away our time and energies and values and physical well-being on what is empty and transitory – and ultimately that is what we end up with. We may look good on the outside, but inside we have nothing...

You know people who have traded in God and God's ways for sex – for drugs – for alcohol – for money – for material things – for pleasure – for leisure... What will become of them? Jesus says it has to be ultimate destruction because the storms WILL come and crush them.

It is up to us to build our lives on those things which are lasting – on a foundation which will not destroy you. IT'S NOT EASY. Building castles in the sand is by far easier – they just don't last.

One last story: A young man was out walking in the woods one winter day, tromping through the snow. He had gone a ways when he heard a noise and knew someone was behind him. He turned and there was a little boy. "What are you doing out here?" he asked. The boy replied, "Please walk carefully, I'm following in your footsteps."

People follow in our footsteps... Another reason to do life right...

Have you been the wise man or the foolish? It's not too late, you know. Your house isn't finished yet. You can still strengthen it and do it right.

FIVE TALENT PEOPLE

1 Corinthians 12:4-11 and Matthew 25:14-27

Jesus looked at him and loved him. "One thing you lack," he said. "Go, sell everything you have and give to the poor, and you will have treasure in heaven. Then come, follow me." At this the man's face fell. He went away sad, because he had great wealth. Jesus looked around and said to his disciples, "How hard it is for the rich to enter the kingdom of God!"

1 Corinthians 12:4-6

Throughout his ministry on earth, Jesus had a number of problems – from Pharisees who opposed him to military leaders who ultimately killed him. But one of the problems that keeps coming up has to do with communication. Jesus wants desperately to tell his followers what the Kingdom of God is like and how to prepare for it and how to make sure they get there. But the mystical Kingdom of God is so "unearthly" – so "phenomenal" – so "non-material" and outside a humans experience that he keeps trying, but never does quite get it across... Much of his teaching begins, "The Kingdom of God is like... " And although the disciples never did grasp it – and we don't either, really – his stories tell other truths that are wonderful lessons in themselves...

The parable we read a few minutes ago is called the "Parable of the Talents." Like so many of the parables, it is trying to say something about the Kingdom of God. I personally don't get a great insight about the Kingdom from the parable... but it's hard to miss the implications about God and God's expectations of His people (maybe that IS the Kingdom of God – God's people meeting God's expectations.).

Anyway – A wealthy and powerful landowner is taking a trip. He is going to be gone for an undisclosed period of time. He might return next week or he might actually be gone for several years... It depends on what he experiences and the success of the trip and how much he feels a longer stay will be worth. He is a businessman and pretty shrewd in his dealings. He hasn't gotten where he is by being always a "nice guy."

He summons three of his most trusted employees and tells them of his upcoming trip. He lets them in on a secret. *All of his wealth is not in his land or in his camels and oxen. Over in the wall safe is a lot of cash.* He doesn't have time before he leaves to invest it and he can't leave it in the house during his absence lest a thief come in, find it, and rob him... And to travel with such a sum would be nothing but foolish.

He goes over to the safe and opens it up and takes out a bag of gold coins that practically fill the whole safe. He says, "I have 8 talents of gold here." (Now, we don't know exactly how much a "talent" was worth. The footnote at the bottom of your Bible says it was more than a thousand dollars. A thousand dollars doesn't seem like such a fortune to us today unless you understand that it wasn't too long ago, even in our own country, that a dollar a day was considered pretty fair wages. Some authorities believe that a talent in Jesus day would have been the equivalent of about 15 years of work for the common laborer... So, if you translate it into earning power, this man pulls out of his safe 8 talents – worth 120 years of a common man's work... If, in our day, the common laborer earns $20,000, we have the equivalent of $2,400,000 he pulls from his safe.) "Now John, you've worked for me for over 20 years. I'm going to put into your keeping 5 talents (a million and a half dollars). "Thomas, you've been with me for a long time too. I'm going to entrust 2 talents to you ($600,000). "Simeon, you've only been with me for 5 years, but you've proved yourself a valuable employee. I'm going to put one talent into your care ($300,000)."

"Listen fellows – I've got to go now. I feel so much better knowing all my money isn't in one spot to be robbed and in the hands of trusted workers. I'll see you later – I don't know just when I'll be back." And he leaves.

So here is John, Thomas, and Simeon with a lot of cash to do something with. John and Thomas took their money and did something with it that ultimately doubled it (I wish the Bible had said what kind of investment doubles one's money – that would be worth a lot, wouldn't it?). But Simeon knows how angry his master will be if he screws this up. He decides to play it safe and wraps it in a plastic bag, places it in a metal box, and buries it under a rock in his back yard where no one would ever find it.

Eventually the master comes home and calls in his employees. They are all beaming with pride. John says, "Look sir. I've doubled what you've given me. Your million and a half dollars is now $3.000,000!" Thomas says, "I've doubled mine too. Here is a million-two!" Simeon, shows no regret. He says, "I wasn't so foolish as to take any chances with your money. I've watched over it and kept it safe. Here is every penny back." *"What, not even simple interest from a savings account? You give me back, after all this time, only what I entrusted you with? You are a fool! You're fired! Get out!"*

I've always thought it interesting that the monetary value of Jesus' parable translates into English as "talent." By so doing, the story takes on all kinds of added meaning. At birth we are each given "talents" by God. We are entrusted with them for 70-80-90 – 100 years, then we take them again and lay them at the feet of God... and if we are wise, we will lay far more down than what we received. We need to ask ourselves how many talents God has given us – only one? – two? – or as many as five? and determine what we are doing with them... I believe most of us want to be a "five talent" person – faithful for the long haul and therefore entrusted with much – and responsible for much...

I couldn't begin to name all the talents present in our congregation. We have musical talents. We have academic talents. We have organizational talents. We have teaching talents. We have serving talents. We have cooking talents. We have leadership talents. We have speaking talents and listening talents and praying talents and encouragement talents... We have all the talents necessary to have the entire body of Christ in our midst. God himself designed our fellowship that way. It is up to each one of us to use and not bury what has been entrusted to us... and it is up to each one of us to be mature enough not to resent someone else's talent nor to think our own superior to someone else's. Ron would not *want* some of us in the choir. Barb Appel would not *want* some of us to teach Sunday School. Terry would not *want* some of us to help keep the financial records straight... But even though some of us cannot sing or teach or keep books, we each *do* have *something* that we can offer to the work of Christ. In fact, it would be ridiculous if we all decided we would like to sing in the choir or teach Sunday School or work in the treasurers office...

Aesop told a fable about an old crow who was out in the wilderness who became thirsty, not having had anything to drink for a couple of days, he was parched and dry and desperately in need of water. He was almost at the end of his strength when he spotted a jug in an old ruins. As he lands and looks into the narrow neck, he sees that it is about half full of water. He reaches in, with his beak, to get a drink.

Unfortunately the neck of the bottle is too narrow for his entire head to fit and the water too far down for his beak to reach it. The jug was too heavy to be tipped by a crow. What could he do? He thought and thought and finally decided on a plan. He began to gather pebbles and drop them, one by one, into the jar. As the jar filled with pebbles, the water rose and eventually he was able to drink his fill...

This is the way of God. The job He has assigned the church is an impossible one. How can we proclaim the good news of Jesus to all the world. It's just too big of a job... But each person of faith, dropping in his or her little pebble, ultimately makes a difference. Each of the little talents shared... each of the hours of time spent... each act of compassion shown... each step of faith taken... added together, do miraculous things.

Maybe you're one of those people who think they have no talents – at least none that could be used for Christ in any significant way... Let's not call them talents, then. Let's call them "opportunities"...

I knew a young woman named Linda many years ago. She had two beautiful daughters but was in a marriage that was just awful. Her husband didn't abuse her but they had gotten married at 17, when they were young and foolish, and over the years, she grew into maturity but he never did. At age 30 he still acted like a 17 year old boy. One day her youngest daughter became suddenly ill – meningitis, I believe it was – and was dead within days. The husband had no ability to be supportive in their grief (he went on a drinking binge) and Linda and Ray eventually got divorced.

Linda surprised me at that point in her life. While she knew she would never fully get over the loss of her daughter, she became more actively involved in her church and began to teach Sunday School (even though she had never done anything like that before) and was elected to the church council and went out and found a job that could support her and her other daughter, got involved in community affairs and has, over the years, accomplished some wonderful things (I believe she was even elected eventually to some public office). I asked her what caused this massive change in her life. She said, "OPPORTUNITY". When her daughter died she realized how fleeting life is and how suddenly it could be gone... She looked at her husband and realized that he had wasted nearly 15 years of his life accomplishing nothing that would last beyond his hang-over. She said she knew she didn't want to end her life (maybe tomorrow) having done nothing of significance – without dropping *her* tiny pebble into the jar, raising the level of the water just a little... She looked around for something to *do* and opportunities were everywhere.

Into each of our lives God has inserted opportunities – so many that it is impossible to take advantage of all of them...

"Welcome back, master. Thank you so much for entrusting those talents to me... Here is what you gave me, and what I've made of it."

What will you lay at the feet of God? What have you done with your entrusted talents?

Seeing the Beauty in Others

Deuteronomy 10:14-21 and Luke 7:1-10.

For the LORD your God is God of gods and Lord of lords, the great God, mighty and awesome, who shows no partiality and accepts no bribes. He defends the cause of the fatherless and the widow, and loves the alien, giving him food and clothing. And you are to love those who are aliens, for you yourselves were aliens in Egypt.
Deuteronomy 10: 17-19

I watched "Titanic" on TV the other night. I had seen it before. I knew what would happen. Yet, I was struck this time by the diversity of people who were on the ship. There were wealthy businessmen, middle-class vacationers, dirt-poor immigrants, stowaways, crew... Young, old, and all ages in between. The class distinction portrayed in the movie apparently was not just Hollywood, and neither was the disproportionate number of survivors. Sixty percent of those in "First-Class" were saved. Forty two percent of those in "Second-Class" survived... and only twenty-five percent of those in "Third Class" lived to tell the story. There is something morally wrong with those statistics. Everyone, no matter what their station in life, is subject to dying – why did so many more "haves" survive than "have-nots"?

There is a tremendous diversity in the body of Christ too. People who call themselves "Christians" are rich, poor, middle class. We come in a variety of colors. The church claims high-school drop-outs and PhD's in its membership. Some work with their hands, others with their minds...some are even unemployed and don't work at all.

We live in a world filled with categories in which to place people. Somehow it makes knowing who you are talking to a little easier... We do it in the church. We call ourselves Baptists or Catholics or Lutherans or Methodists or Congregationalists. And I suppose there is nothing wrong with that so long as we realize that we are all sons and daughters of the same God and that we all call Jesus "Lord" and don't get too hung up on our doctrinal and stylistic differences and think they make any difference, really – that if you don't believe just like me or if you don't worship like I do or if you don't baptize in the same manner as we do, we have no fellowship with one another... God made a wonderful diversity of people – we differ in the ways we think and react and speak and believe... and it's really a wonderful thing.

But, while diversity is good, division is bad. There are enough division points among people in the world without it happening in the church. Fashion consultants have identified the four seasons of the year to distinguish the color of clothing people look best in. I think I'm a "winter." Psychologists give tests, like the "Myers-Briggs" to determine the different personality types and assign each of us a letter. Teachers use letter grades to let students know what category of academic excellence they have fallen into... It seems like everything we do and everywhere we go we is labeled...

Jesus broke with the conventions of cultural categorization. He shattered stereotypes of "us" and "them." He saw every person as created in the image of God. He believed each person – no matter what the circumstances of income, color, status or education – was equal.

Just think of the culturally acceptable categories Jesus disregarded. He considered children as worthy of his time and attention, even going so far as saying that unless adults become like them they couldn't get into heaven... Children, even not too long ago, were to be seen and not heard. In Jesus day, for an adult – especially a man – to hold children in high regard was unheard-of.

Jesus actually touched lepers. He ate with "sinners." He taught Gentiles. He welcomed women in his band of followers... The disciples who walked with Jesus for three years *thought* they knew who they were, but as they spent time with him, the labels of their lives began to fall off...

A couple of weeks ago we talked about the Samaritan woman Jesus talked to at the well. She was an outcast in her own community, which was, in itself, a lower-caste of Judaism... But Jesus talked with her and showed he cared... The disciples, died-in-the-wool orthodox Jews, didn't know what to think of this.

When most of us think of prejudice, we think in terms of race. And for good reason. The inhumane treatment of African Americans and Native Americans and other ethnic groups is not just a thing of the past, it happens every day. I was embarrassed a couple of years ago when I read or heard the statement that "11:00 on any Sunday morning is the most segregated hour in America." I was embarrassed because I knew it was true. Christians, all of whom claim to have the same heavenly father, seek out people like themselves and sometimes work very hard to exclude others.

But race is just one of the issues. It is constantly before us, so it springs to mind. I know people who practically hate obese people. Perhaps they, themselves, have a tendency toward being over-weight and work at it diligently – and resent those who don't have the determination.

Others look down on the homeless. It's not pity or sympathy, it is looking down on them as though they are of less value.

The thing is, each one of us have our own prejudices. We have irrational dislikes for others we have labeled others in a certain way – sometimes we even know the characterization is inaccurate or inappropriate. Or he label may actually be accurate, but our response to it is un-Christlike.

I've put a little flier in each of your bulletins today. I call it a "Prejudice Picker." It is simply for the purpose of thinking through some of the attitudes in your heart that are not very "Christian." You don't have to write anything in the blanks. In fact, I encourage you NOT to. But do fill in the blanks in your mind... Let's look at it.

Statement #1: I feel superior whenever I am around a(n) _____ (African American, Native American, Asian, Hispanic, Caucasian, Third World refugee, etc.)

This is a natural tendency. If you feel superior around some ethnic group, you are pretty much like everyone else... But that is a wrong feeling. You (I) are NOT superior. We are each created in the image of God and loved equally by Him. Who do we think we are to feel superior? Can you learn to appreciate ethnic differences? Yes, you can. But it may be possible initially only as you view them in the light of God's love.

Statement #2: I'm sure glad I'm not going to be in _____ shoes when Judgment Day comes. (People with AIDS, alcoholics, homosexuals, drug users, prostitutes, TV evangelists, politicians, etc.)

It is virtually impossible to separate the sin from the sinner as humans... But that is exactly what God expects of his children. Can you love the "low lifes" of this world? Only by the grace of God are you NOT one.

Statement #3: When I follow my natural inclinations, I tend to avoid _____. (Children, teenagers, those divorced, the handicapped, the elderly, those who attend a church unlike ours, short people, etc.)

People in some categories make us uncomfortable. Why?

Statement #4: I have difficulty accepting _____ in places of leadership at work or at church. (Women, men, youth, those less educated, new Christians, the self-confident, the shy, etc.)

Statement #5: Unless my son or daughter marries a _____ I will be very unhappy. (College graduate, lifelong Protestant, native of an English-speaking country, Republican, Democrat, Congregationalist, person of his or her own age. etc.)

What can you observe about yourself from the way you filled in the blanks? Are you surprised at some of your responses? Would you say you are more prone to lump people together in groups than to see them as individuals?

Jesus opened the eyes of his disciples to their stereotypes – to their prejudices... People were drawn to Jesus because he saw the beauty in others – in individuals, not in groups...

In Luke 7, a Roman centurion came to Jesus on behalf of his servant. The servant was deathly ill and it was clear he would die soon... Jesus surprises his onlookers by treating this Gentile with the same courtesy and respect as he would a fellow Jew.

Here was a Roman soldier. The Romans were the rulers of the land but despised by non-Romans. Jews wanted nothing to do with them. They were dogs. They were the minions of that autocrat, Caesar...

The centurion loved his servant and had heard that Jesus was a great healer. The soldier found some Jewish elders and asked them to speak to Jesus to see if he might come and heal the servant. He didn't expect that he would. He could have commanded it, of course, but that would not have been right – can you "force" a healer to heal?

Jesus headed immediately for the centurion's home. When He spotted Jesus coming, he sent a message: "Jesus, thank you for coming, but please don't come into my house. I know it would defile you and your followers wouldn't approve (Jews were not allowed to enter the home of ANY Gentile, lest they be polluted and become unclean). But if you would just speak the word from where you are, I know Hermes will be healed."

Jesus was astounded at that message. He turned to his true-blue, died-in-the-wool purebred disciples and said, "In the whole of Israel – among God's own people – I have never encountered such faith! Can you see what just may be beyond your prejudices... There may be people who put your own faith to shame."

We have a neighbor who moved in a couple of years ago who caused everyone on the block to talk. He is a huge fellow, dark skinned, tattooed, always wearing black leather. Parked in front of his house is often a huge motorcycle... The wife is a bleached blond. As soon as they moved in they put a couple of great big dog statues at the entrance to their driveway – not poodles – Dobermans, I think. He is often out walking his dog. Sue thinks it is a Pit Bull – I'm not sure, but it isn't a friendly looking beast.

I decided one sunny summer afternoon to go get acquainted when I saw him out working on his "hog." I discovered a genuinely nice person – and I heard Mary, his wife, inside listening to Christian music. I discovered they attend church every Sunday except when they are out with their motorcycle club on tours. Then the group holds its own worship time. He is some kind of engineer with an automotive feeder company.... It turned out that Dan and Mary are warm and wonderful Christian people...

Here is your assignment for this week: Take a walk through your neighborhood and allow Jesus to walk with you. Walk with an attitude of prayer, silently talking to God about people you may not even know. The houses you will pass will hold mysteries for you. But you will know, simply on the basis of statistical studies that people *that house* may well be concerned for a family member with cancer. Another might have a son or daughter heading in the wrong direction in life. Another family might be struggling to hold a difficult marriage together... Pray for each of them, even though you don't know specific needs – know that every one of those homes hold families who DO have needs... Pray God's protection and peace on every home. Ask God to bring people into their lives who can show them the love of God. Tell God you are willing to be that person, if He wants and if the opportunity arises...

I've heard of a man who gets up every morning with the same prayer, " God, I'm available. Show me who needs You most today."

People you meet every day are God's children. Jesus wants us to, as much as possible, put aside our prejudices and stereotypes and love others – to see each individual not as a "group" to be judged, but as a person Jesus died to save...

WHY THEY HATE US – AND WHAT WE CAN DO ABOUT IT

Micah 6:6-8 and Matthew 25:31-40.

Will the LORD be pleased with thousands of rams, with ten thousand rivers of oil? Shall I offer my firstborn for my transgression, the fruit of my body for the sin of my soul?
Micah 6:7

Four hundred years before Jesus walked the earth, there was a sect of philosophers in Greece known as "Sophists." They were men who prided themselves on their ability to convince anyone of anything. They employed logic and rationalization and complicated analogies – whatever it took to win their debate... They pointed out the flaws in their opponents reasoning – they were committed to NEVER losing.

Of course, in those days, there were no TV's or radio's or newspapers. There weren't even books that the average person could get access to. For entertainment, people would flock to hear lecturers on just about any subject (they preferred the traveling minstrels and acrobats – they weren't any more intellectually astute than we are – but whatever show came to town, crowds would appear).

And the Sophists would put on quite a show. They weren't terribly interested in the truth, they were interested in the fine art of persuasion. They boasted of their ability to make the bad seem good and that they could actually convince the multitudes that black was, in reality, white.

As their "act" continued on over the course of years, they put a new spin on it. They would do a two night (day?) show, then move on to the next town. The first night they would take a position – on politics or law or ethics or science or religion – and thoroughly convince the crowd of their way of thinking. They would so enthuse the audience that people would cheer and applaud and become life-long devotes to that position. A few days later they would put on their second lecture of the series – but this time thoroughly convince the same crowd of the opposite position.

You can imagine the confusion in the minds and hearts of the listeners... Their "teachers" – these wise and learned men – were able to control them as though they were puppets!

The human spirit can take only so much of that kind of thing. Within a short time, the Sophist party disappeared from the earth. The people, enraged at being so humiliated, rose up and killed them.

After 9-11 President Bush asked the question, "Why do they hate us?" Then he answered his own question by saying it is because "they hate our freedoms."

President Bush spoke before thinking. Nobody hates freedom... not even terrorists. They hate us because we, as a nation, are the Sophists of the modern world. We are able to convince ourselves and much of the world that we are right no matter what we say or do. We are able to portray ourselves as a "Christian" nation, but then adopt policies and take actions that are just the opposite of what "Christian" means.

Right here at home:

- We sing "God Bless America" with passion...but at the same time believe there should be NOTHING of God in our schools or in our communities. (Did you know that right here in Livonia, on the official internet website for the city, where the city tries to show how great it is and how much it has to offer, the only church, apparently, in town, is at Greenmeade?)
- We go to church more than any nation on earth, but also crank out more pornography and smut and pollution for the minds of the world than anyone. We proclaim morality, but everything you see on TV or the movies says otherwise...
- We truly believe we are a peace-loving country, but cannot count on all of our fingers the number of wars or conflicts in which we've dropped bombs – just in this generation.

- We advocate human rights as a high ideal, yet perform more abortions than can be counted each year... ...we hold back minorities whenever we can get away with it... ...we refuse to provide health care, when we have the ability to do so, to people who desperately need it.
- We proclaim religious freedom but look askance at turbans and veils and robes and shaven heads...wondering why they can't be more like good, American Christians...

The fact of the matter is, the world can't escape us. America and Americans are everywhere. If you take a trip to Europe – Eastern or Western; to Australia; to China; to Africa; to the Middle East – you find McDonalds and The Gap and blue jeans and rock-and-roll music – you find people speaking English on just about every street corner... And *people who care about their religion and their culture* (both going back hundreds or thousands of years before there even WAS an America) **resent it.**

They <u>love</u> our freedom – they don't hate it ...*but who we are and how we use our freedom and our power scares them senseless.* We are the teen-age boy who has, virtually overnight, outgrown his peers and his siblings and even his parents. He is discovering his new power and finds he doesn't have to respect anyone anymore. He is a sophomore! His ways are the right ways and he is willing to convince you of it however he has to do it.

I love America. I have no doubt in my mind whatsoever that God has blessed us as he has blessed no nation on earth – including the "chosen" nation of Israel. We have the best nation that exists, or perhaps has ever existed, on earth. I believe that so long as we strive to follow the principles laid out in the 10 Commandments and so long as we don't forsake the principles of Jesus, that blessing will continue.

Hatred in the world is not there by nature. It comes from somewhere. Resentment has root causes... and as much as we hate to give the terrorists an inkling of credibility, SOMETHING causes them to do what they do. Would YOU give up your life in a violent, horrible death if there wasn't SOMETHING you were trying to say? ...Something that was making you crazy?

There are disenchanted and disenfranchised and poor and hungry and oppressed people all over the world. THEY don't bomb buildings with passenger filled airplanes... only mad men do that – only the most deranged fanatics do that – only men who have sold out to evil do that. If you or I hate something or someone or even some nation, we would never consider terrorist tactics. That is unforgivable... The vast majority of the Arab world – whether they like us or not, would never CONSIDER terrorist activity... And I'm not sure they like us any more than the terrorists... The only consolation is that most of the Arab world also hates dictators like Saddam Hussein and the Ayatollah who take away their freedoms and keep them in ignorance and poverty and make them "worship" themselves and kill them if they speak out...

BUT the underlying question remains – WHY?

Peter Ford, in an article in the "Christian Science Monitor" quotes an Arab man: "...[What is] the motivation behind the assault on New York and Washington? The motivation is everywhere... When a president stands up before the planet and says an American comes first, he is only preaching hatred. When a president stands up and says we don't honor our missile treaty with the Russians, he is only preaching arrogance. When he refuses to condemn what's happening in Palestine, he is only preaching tyranny... American foreign policy has invited everybody, actually, to try to humiliate America, and to give it a bloody nose..."

It's like the bully on the play ground. It doesn't really matter whether he has done anything to you or not, if you see someone go after him, there is never any question who you root for...

I love Israel. You all know that. But Israel is a splinter in the palm of the Middle East, and throughout the Middle East everyone knows that Israel, without America, is nothing. We supply their F-16's and M-16's and Apache helicopters whereby they not only defend themselves, but take aggressive action while we turn our heads, pretending they are completely innocent – even the aggrieved party... It is true that they are a gnat on the camel in terms of population and size and that without help from some quarter they would be squashed instantly. And I am glad we are the ones helping them survive. I hope we never forsake them... But to convince ourselves that Israel is an innocent – is sophistry.

They hate us because what we do seems to contradict who we say we are... On major issues we contradict our own ethical and moral values and convince ourselves that we haven't. We give money and weapons to "freedom fighters" in developing countries around the world so they can overthrow their own governments but insist that terrorism is wrong... (If I'm not mistaken, it was US who helped get Saddam in power in the first place...) It's a hard policy to defend, but somehow, in our sophisticated thinking, we can do it... but many in the world see through our twisted logic and it scares them – as well it should.

They hate us because we are a "Christian" nation. They don't hate Christians because we follow Christ. They hate us because our religion is so terribly weak... because we DON'T follow Christ – for the most part even the true Christians. Our faith has no real influence on the world or on our own nation's policies or on society or even on our individual lives... We lack commitment to our faith... For the Muslim that is absurd. True faith demands sacrifice and discipline and morality. They are required to pray six times each day. They fast during daylight hours for an entire month every year. They forbid alcoholic beverages, premarital sex, and failure to worship... Interestingly, our own faith demands discipline and morality and prayer and even suggests the benefits of fasting.... We abhor alcoholism and forbid premarital sex and believe that "Remembering the Sabbath to keep it Holy" is one of our major rules... But we wink at all of those, don't we?

This "Christian" thing, to them, is simply playing at religion and no self-respecting god would give us the time of day...

Can you imagine what American culture represents to a young Muslim who, outside of his family, has never seen a woman's knee, or even her face? Philip Yancey writes, "Much of the world draws conclusions about 'the Christian West' from MTV, Baywatch, and violent movies. Muslims speak of nuclear weapons as 'the Christian bomb.'"

At this very moment, the leaders of the United States are trying to decide whether to go out and make war with Iraq. Why? Because we fear them. We fear what the makers and formers of that culture are capable of... Don't you see – they fear us (and hate us) for the same reasons... THEY hate us because we are godless. They hate us because we are a decadent, corrupt, dangerous people.

They hate us because our religion and religious beliefs are dictated by our government and American policies and interests... Some of you sitting here this morning are card-carrying Republicans. Others are died-in-the wool Democrats. I want to say to you today that NEITHER party represents the principles of Jesus Christ and that HIS is the party we, as Christians, must belong to. We must support policies that He would support and resist those He would resist. He called us the salt and light of the world and warned that when the salt no longer makes a difference and when the light is no longer shining, we are no good in society any longer...

Did you listen to the words of the prophet Micah this morning?

"What does the Lord require of you? To act justly and to love mercy and to walk humbly with your God." When you find a politician with THOSE values – ones who ACT justly – ones who LOVE mercy – and ones who walk humbly, you can support him or her as a Christian. But they are rare...

Jesus has a vision in Matthew 25. He sees all the nations of the earth gathered around him and He is about to judge them. Those He judges as righteous will be those who feed the hungry of the world, whose who go out of their way to sustain life, who make sure the poor have clothing and food and the sick have health care... And he goes a step further. He condemns any nation which doesn't do these things. Even a sophist can't reinterpret those words – all he can do is ignore them..........

You and I – American Christians – need to be standing against that which Jesus stands against and for what he stands for... giving time to food kitchens, giving money to organizations like Prison Fellowship International and World Vision and the Salvation Army and the International Justice Mission which demonstrate in concrete ways what WE believe are true "Western Values" – "Christian Values" are all about. ... How differently would the world view us if it associated the U.S. with Jesus rather than Baywatch – Jesus rather than capitalism – Jesus rather than anything...

May God bless America... and may America be a blessing to the world as HIS truth goes marching on.

THE CHURCH IN AMERICA

Deuteronomy 12:5-7 and Revelation 14:6-7; 15:3b-4

But you are to seek the place the LORD your God will choose from among all your tribes to put his Name there for his dwelling. To that place you must go; 6 there bring your burnt offerings and sacrifices, your tithes and special gifts, what you have vowed to give and your freewill offerings, and the firstborn of your herds and flocks. 7 There, in the presence of the LORD your God, you and your families shall eat and shall rejoice in everything you have put your hand to, because the LORD your God has blessed you.
Deuteronomy 12: 5-7

It is truly good to be back at Mt. Hope for the past couple of weeks. It's good to stand here in the pulpit. It's good to look out there and see faces I've grown to love during the past two decades....

I church hopped last spring and summer (for those of you who weren't here or didn't otherwise know, I had an awesome 17 week sabbatical that concluded August 17). If you remember, when I left, I urged you to attend church even though your minister would be gone and promised you that I would do the same whenever I was in an English speaking country. I had the wonderful opportunity to attend 10 or so different churches. That may not seem like such a "cool" thing to you – you can do that sort of thing any time you want. But for a minister, seeing what goes on "out there" in other churches is eye opening and often quite inspirational. I attended a couple of Congregational Churches, a Lutheran church, a contemporary non-denominational church, a Presbyterian Church, an Evangelical Free Church, and even a Greek Orthodox Church. I was looking for variety – I was looking for inspiration – I was looking for ideas – ...I was looking, most of all, for God.

I have little doubt that God was in each of the places I visited. All around me were people who were there because they wanted to be. It was summer – the perfect excuse for skipping church. Unless you somehow find peace there or inspiration or comfort or forgiveness or acceptance or friendship... or God, there is no reason to go... The churches I attended didn't always worship in a way that resonated with my spirit, but there are a great variety of people in this world and a great many ways of expressing love and devotion to God. I know that and I respect it.

Then I came back to Mt. Hope and found the place I wanted to be more than any of the others... For me, THIS is where God is (although God was pretty awesomely present during my stay in the Austrian Alps too).

While I was "out there" in other churches, I saw some interesting things and made some observations. I saw, more clearly than at any time in the past 20 years, some of our own church's weaknesses and places where we might need to bolster our ministry.

There was one very noticeable thing that happened in every one of the churches I visited. Except at the two Congregational Churches where some people knew us, we weren't greeted by anyone except the usher who was handing out the bulletins. NO ONE! – Not one person at any of the churches we visited went out of their way to make us feel welcome! ...And I tried. At the church I considered my "favorite" (don't ask, I won't tell you which one I liked best – I don't want you to try it out and like it too and leave us), I arrived a few minutes early, sat in a row with others, participated in worship (they did have one of those "stand up, turn to your neighbor and greet one another" times and a couple of people did say good-morning then – but not after the service. After the service even the ones who greeted me during the greeting time treated me like I was invisible). After worship I intentionally stood alone in the narthex, stopped and read the bulletin boards, slowly walked among chatting people, **tried my best** to get **someone** to greet and welcome me – to ask my name or whether I was a first-time visitor. Mission *impossible*.

Now, I imagine that, if I had taken the initiative and struck up a conversation with someone, he or she would have responded and been quite pleasant and we'd have gotten along just fine... But it takes a pretty self-confident visitor to do such a thing.

I was pretty sure that experience could never happen at Mt. Hope. I hope I am right. The church needs to be a welcoming place for anyone who walks through the doors. Not to bolster our numbers, but because that is what Jesus would have us be... it says, "Jesus lives in us" to strangers. And if He does, then he needs to shine out of us too.

It's good to come to church to see your friends – to chat and share your past week's experiences with them – to laugh and enjoy. But if you shut out the stranger in your midst, something is terribly wrong.

Like I said, I don't think that happens here... And I also think that when a visitor does grace our sanctuary, they are greeted, not out of obligation, but because the greeter really is glad a visitor has come and wants to get a bit acquainted and wants to make sure he/she/they feel welcome...

But welcome or not, a lot of people go to church on Sunday mornings. I was terribly impressed with the size of most of the churches I attended. LOTS of people, even in the summer months (A/C no doubt bolsters attendance everywhere). At one of the churches – the Orthodox one – I was shocked at how few people there were when I walked in and took a seat. But then I found out a secret. No one actually comes on time in the Orthodox church. By the end of the service, the handful of worshippers had become 400-500 (and since the service is at least a couple of hours long, that works).

One church I attended because I received a postcard that I found offensive. I guess that says that any publicity is good publicity. Normally you'd think you WOULDN'T go to a place that offended you – but curiosity got the best of me. [Display the postcard, "Going to church doesn't have to be BOOORRRING!"]. Clearly they are trying to "steal sheep" as we call it in the ministry – get members of other churches to join theirs. Their not-so-subtle suggestion is that the traditional church is deadly dull – no place you'd want to be... and certainly no place you'd take your children if you have any sense at all... Well, being the pastor of a "traditional" church, I thought this about as tacky as you can get. Sue and I went to see what was so great about this church.

It was comfortably full – probably 7-800 people there. They had a rock band, they did a skit, they flashed the words of the songs on big projection screens, the minister gave a very nice lecture on marriage, they even did 15 baptisms...

Ironically, there was a little boy sitting in front of us who played his Gameboy for about 45 minutes until he got bored with that and fell asleep just like the little boy on their postcard.

I had to keep asking myself everywhere I went – "What is the appeal of this church? Why are there so many people here? Why do these churches grow and Mt. Hope and thousands of other churches don't – or at least seem to hit a ceiling and stop growth at that point?" I've wanted our church to grow. I've worked at that for 20 years. It has grown – more than double the size it was 20 years ago, but we don't have 1000 people – or 500 –or even 400… Some of these churches gather huge numbers in an incredibly short time. Why? What is it? Where are we defective?

I've concluded that **_it's not the minister_**. The men I heard were nothing exceptional. Most of them just a few years out of seminary. With a couple of them I had a hard time staying awake… I like to think I do at least as well as they do….

It's not the music that makes them grow large. Generally speaking, the singing was terrible. The special music was mediocre. The music was usually so loud that the congregation doesn't sing or the songs are too unfamiliar for them to sing, so they don't… My journal entry includes this sentence: "I attended this service alone and came home and said to Sue that I'd never criticize Mt. Hope singing again…"

It's not the warmth of the people. When you get a thousand or so people together it's somewhat like going to a movie. You enter and you exit without ever speaking to the stranger next to you. That's OK. That's expected and acceptable.

And, interestingly, **_I don't think growth has much to do with theology_**. One church I attended was borderline Unitarian, another used to be called Baptist. One was Lutheran and one was Evangelical… I'm not saying God isn't a factor. I'm saying that what the people believe and what the minister preaches doesn't seem to be a factor…

I've been asking that question for the past two decades. *What is it that makes some churches grow huge and other churches not?* If it's not the minister, not the music, not the people, not the theology – and certainly not the building, what is it???

I've suspected, as I've talked with some of my colleagues of churches like Mt. Hope, that it has to do with programs. Large churches can offer grief counseling groups, organized basketball teams, singles groups… a group for this and a group for that. If you have a need, they have a group or a specialty minister on their staff who can meet it. But I don't think it's programming, either.

Then, last week, Barbara Chenot handed me the answer to my ministry-long question without ever knowing it. She gave me an article from a church newsletter that she had gotten from somewhere. It looked interesting so I read it.

It talked about a conference their minister had attended on church growth. It suggested that he had learned that there are four basic categories of churches in terms of size and growth. Your size depends on what kind of church you are or work at being...

– A church with an average Sunday attendance of 0 - 50 adults is considered a "Family" church. I'm not sure exactly how they define that term, but it must essentially mean that a very small church is made up of a few families and they pretty much control whatever goes on there in a totally democratic kind of way. Pastors come and go, but the families stay for generations. So it's called a "Family" church.

– A church with an average Sunday attendance of 51-200 adults is classified as a "Pastoral" church. The people know and respect the pastor. He/she tends to have a big voice in what goes on in the congregation...

– A church of 201-400 adults in attendance is called a "Program" church – that means they have made a conscious effort to offer a myriad of programs for the people...

– A church of 401- ??? is known as a "Corporate" church.

As I looked at those designations and thought about them, the phone rang. It was one of you. "Steve, my grandfather is in the ICU. He's not doing well..."

"I'll be there in 15 minutes..."

And I knew. A Corporate church is a place like a corporation. It is run by professionals and run like a business. You never actually see the powers-that-be. It's just big and... "corporate." Maybe it's even on TV... Everyone's heard of it. There's a certain pride in going there... It's a great place. It's "professional" grade.

The "Program" church has become large enough that committees and a ministerial staff make the decisions for the whole. A single minister simply can't handle everything alone. Too many people. Too many obligations. Too many things to juggle. He begins to separate from the congregation. He **has** to be less available because there is simply too much to do. Most of the people of the congregation would recognize their minister on the street, but would never approach him – any more than they would if they saw the mayor or the school superintendent or the chief of police. Not that they couldn't, there just would be no point. He would *maybe* recognize you – maybe not. They have moved beyond the pastoral calling to provide programs for the saints. It's a great thing. No more boring church. There are things to learn. Things to do. Meetings to attend. A dazzling worship service. There truly is joy in numbers!

"Steve, my daughter is pregnant. Can she come and talk to you?" "Steve, did you know that Sally is in the hospital. She'd appreciate a visit." "Hi Pastor Steve. I've got a problem…" "Pastor Schafer, would you be willing to give communion to our residents here at the retirement center each month?" "Steve, do you know of a book that I can read that will help me understand the Muslim religion?" "Pastor Steve, my little son Timmy, wants to be baptized. Can you explain it to him?"

And I knew why Mt. Hope can never become a huge church. We put a high value on the pastoral touch. The people of Mt. Hope and hundreds of thousands of churches like Mt. Hope value being called by name by the minister and by people in the church family. It is important to be able to call your minister "friend" – to call him in time of need or sorrow or joy… Why would anyone WANT to be labeled a "Corporate" church? What is the appeal of the label "Program" church? Why, in our world of corporations and programs and slick advertising and impersonalness would anyone choose anything but a "Pastoral" congregation?

Does Mt. Hope need to grow this year? Of course it does. We've all heard of that little phrase of Jesus called the "Great Commission." They were his last words on earth: "Go into all the world and make disciples of all peoples, baptizing them in the name of the Father and of the Son and of the Holy Spirit…and I will be with you until the end of the age." There are plenty of people out there looking for us – people without a church – people who need Jesus Christ in their lives – people who need to know people who love God.

There is plenty of room here for them. We haven't grown beyond the "Pastoral" size yet. When we get there, we'll need to make some decisions. But until then, Jesus urges us to go into all the world – into our neighborhoods and into our workplaces and wherever in our world needy people are – and bring them in to meet our Lord.

Whose Fries Are These, Anyway?

Matthew 19:17-21 and 1 Chronicles 29:10 -18.

But who am I, and who are my people, that we should be able to give as generously as this? Everything comes from you, and we have given you only what comes from your hand.

1 Chronicles 29:14

I've got another story about that same little boy in last week's sermon and his dad... As you recall, little Timmy is 6 years old and he and his dad have a special relationship. Last week they went fishing, this week they are taking a leisurely week-end at home. Dad has been doing some handy-man tasks around the house and Timmy is helping him out. It gets to be about noon and dad says, "Timmy, you've been a great help today. You've worked hard and I've really appreciated it (that's what all good dads say to their 6 year olds who 'help' with jobs even though dad could probably have gotten the whole thing done quicker without any help at all – it's the relationship that counts, not the actual amount of the help). So what would you like for lunch?"

"I've been thinking of McDonald's fries. I'd LOVE to have some." So dad and Timmy get into the car and head for the nearest McDonald's. They go in and sit down and dad goes to the counter to get some fries for Timmy. But he doesn't order just a regular fry. Timmy hears him order a "super size" fry instead and is delighted. Dad pulls out his wallet, hands the clerk a $20 and waits for his change. Dad brings the fries and a large Coke back to the table and sets them in front of Timmy.

Timmy's dad had taught him that we ought to thank God for our food, so Timmy immediately bows his head and, because the fries smell so wonderful, says a quick prayer, "God, bless this food. Amen."

Dad is happy to see his little boy so happy over something so simple. He decides to join in the fun. He reaches over to get a couple of Timmy's fries.

To his surprise, his son quickly puts his arms around his fries as though building a fort and pulls them toward himself and says, "No, these are mine." His dad was in a state of shock for a moment. He could not believe what had just happened…

Dad pulls back his hand and begins to reflect about his son's attitude… Here's what went through his mind:

1. My son failed to realize that I am the source of those French fries. Without me, he couldn't even have gotten here…

2. At the counter, I was the one who gave the cashier the money from my wallet. I paid for them – 100%

3. I did not give him the size fry he was expecting, but something twice as big. Yet here he is talking about them being his French fries as though they really are.

4. Not only was I the source of the French fries, he has forgotten that I, at 6ft 1 and 195 lbs, have the power to take all the fries I might wannt despite his little arms surrounding them as a fort. …Or that if I wanted to, I could go back to the counter and bring him so many fries that he could never eat them all….

5. He also doesn't understand, that I don't need his French fries. I could go back to the counter and get as many fries as I wanted for myself.

As the Dad thought about it, one or two fries really wouldn't have made much of a difference for him that day. The fries were insignificant. What he wanted was for his son Jimmy, to invite him into the wonderful little world he had made possible for his son. He wanted his son to be willing to share the pleasure that he had provided… and it was incomprehensible that he wouldn't.

In our lives, God takes you and me, his children, to McDonald's on a regular basis. God blesses us. He blesses you and He blesses me. He's given us all some French Fries – more than we've asked for… Some have small bags, others medium, others large and some super size. Some are narrow and light in color like McDonald's, others are thick and dark like Rally's. Some are straight and some are Arby's curly fries. But God has given each one of us some fries.

Like that Dad, God desires to sit down at the table with us for some fellowship. But when God reaches over to use some of the blessings he has given to us, far too often we say "No God, these are mine. No, No, No. Go and get your own." We try building our own little forts around our blessings as though those blessings really belonged to us in some natural way...

Is there anybody here this morning that truly understands that God is the source of all that we receive? Sure we go out there every day and work for our wages (much like Timmy did, working for his dad), but how many of us realize that we've got to have something within us that we didn't put there that makes that work possible and that we, in ourselves don't' even have the ability to get up and go to work?

Is there anybody here today that understands that God has the ability to take away everything we think is ours and that God has the ability to give us far more than what we have? There's not a single person here today who knows how many times God has already spared their lives when death came knocking. We should never underestimate God's power to protect us from things we did not even know about.

Is there anybody here that recognizes God does not need our French fries, and that it is an honor and a privilege to be able to share our fries with God? God does not ask us to give because God is hurting and in desperate need. God asks us to give because God wants us to be like Him. God has a giving attitude and he wants that giving attitude modeled in his children. The first verse many people learn is John 3:16 which begins, for God so love the world that he what... He *gave* His only Son...

Throughout the Bible, you find that God is always giving. In our own lives, how many of us know that we cannot underestimate God's ability to provide for us even when we don't give the proper thanks? God is intensely interested in our response to the blessings He sends our way and what we choose to do with them.

Let's look at the passage of Scripture in 1 Chronicles we read this morning...

In the first nine verses (the part of the chapter we didn't read), the Israelites had just taken up an incredible offering for a new building project. They were going to build the first temple for God. The people had gone crazy in their giving. They were giving their jewelry and the gold from their ornamental furnishings around the house, they were giving their coins and their family heirlooms – they were going to build God a temple unlike the world had ever seen... They had a vision for what God had done for them and they wanted to do something for God that reflected that...

The passage we read this morning is a prayer of King David, and it points out some important things:

1. He suggests that the people KNOW that all things in heaven and on earth belong to God. A good starting point... a knowledge that has belonged to all reasonable people from the beginning of time... "...everything in heaven and earth are yours... Wealth and honor come from you; you are the ruler of all things. In your hands are strength and power to exalt and give strength to all."

2. Then David goes on to say something we seldom consider: "But who am I, and who are my people, that we should be able to give as generously as this? Everything comes from you, and we have given you only what comes from your hand. We are aliens and strangers... Our days on earth are like a shadow, without hope. O LORD our God, as for all this abundance that we have provided for building you a temple for your Holy Name, it comes from your hand, and all of it belongs to you [anyway]."

David sees the absurdity of giving to God. He says, "Look God, I'm little Timmy. How can I presume to be proud to give you what is already yours? Really, I'm nothing. I'm just a poor little kid who depends on your handouts. I'm just YOUR little kid who doesn't even realize that what I'm getting IS a handout..."

Whether we worked for it, won it, found it, or received it as a gift. God is still the ultimate source. Everything we even think we own, belongs to God. Our cars, Our houses, Our video games, Our clothes, Our jewelry and even our food belongs to God. Your health, your family, your loved ones – all a gift from God...Without God's grace, we have nothing. ...Doesn't it amaze you that we would act like Timmy with the French fries with God.

God gives us all these French fries and we're sitting around saying, "Oh no, no, no these are mine!" God, as a parent, is hurt because we have such a limited understanding of the fact that everything we have was God's and still is God's. ...If you really think something belongs to you, die and try to keep somebody else from taking it.

In the book of Malachi, God asked the people to bring in a tithe and see if He would not bless them for it. A tithe is nothing more than a penny out of a dime, or a dime out of dollar.

If God sat with you at a table, and gave you 10 dimes, what would cause you to say no if God asked for one of them back? Yet 90% of all people who say they love God will say, "No God, this is mine."

We get uptight about even hearing of giving 10% when God is entitled to the full 100% to do as He pleases. Strange, isn't it, that the moment God puts money into our hands, we declare, "this is mine. I'll only give what I want to give." Up goes the fortress around our fries. We have no idea of how blessed we are and of all the things that God has done for us... we are as six year old children.

Some of us would like to show God our gratitude, but, like Timmy, we're not sure we will have enough fries to meet all your needs and desires.

There are three things we should know about God when we are afraid to believe that God will meet our needs financially if we become tithers. The first deals with God's power. By this I mean God's ability. Does God have the ability to give us what we need if we give to the work of God in this life?

If we can believe Jesus, it does. We trust Jesus with our eternal salvation which is by far the greatest thing we have at stake. This same Jesus told us in our New Testament reading today, "anyone who gives up anything or any relationship for the gospel sake will receive up to a hundred times as much and will inherit eternal life."

This is the same Jesus that took five loaves of bread and two fish and fed over 5000 people. If Jesus could do this with a little boy's lunch, can't he provide what YOU need?

"Lord, if after I pay for cable, call waiting, three way calling, designer clothing, a car, and last year's Christmas shopping on my credit cards..., if there's anything left, I'll show you my love. But right now don't reach over here for 10% of my fries."

Anything that God asks of you, God has made it possible for you to do. Is there anyone here who would ask their child to go to the store and purchase some milk, knowing that the milk would cost $2.99 but you only gave them .50? No. If you expected them to bring home milk, you'd give them enough money to do it.

I find it fascinating that most people always want to give God something they don't have. "Lord If I had a million dollars, I would give a chunk of it to the church to alleviate the budget crunch... But God says, "No. You keep the chunk you would have given if you had a million, but let's talk about the $450 check you do get every week or every two weeks or once a month. I'd rather have that $45 which tells me, 'go ahead and eat some of my fries... I want you to be a part of the joy and abundance in my life.'"

The only time God asks us to test Him is when it comes to our giving back to Him. God isn't asking us to become poor. God is asking us to become rich... He isn't asking us to give all we have. He is asking us to give PART of what He has given us so He can feel good about give us all we want and need...

(Malachi 3:10-12) "'Bring the whole tithe into the storehouse, that there may be food in my house. Test me in this,'" says the LORD Almighty, "'and see if I will not throw open the floodgates of heaven and pour out so much blessing that you will not have room enough for it.'"

God's word is saying that we can all afford to tithe. It does not say we can all afford to tithe and hold on to everything we have. You see, some of us have been spending God's money so long on the wrong things that we might have to let some of them go and begin to get our finances in order. Maybe we have to let go of the premium channels on cable, or our obsession with always driving a brand new car or spending a fortune at restaurants... Maybe God has been paying for some of your luxuries a bit too long. Tithing is simply a matter of choosing to do what we ought to do in our relationship with the Jesus.

We serve a giving God. The more we serve Him, the more giving we should become. Will you break down your wall around your fries and say to God, "Heavenly father, your plan and your purposes for my life and the lives of those around me, are far greater than what I could do with these fries. You take a few of them and do as you please."

In your bulletin this morning, you should have found an "Intention of Giving" card and an envelope just like the one you received in the mail this week. I hope you have discussed it with your family and decided what God is calling you to give this year... and I hope you've considered tithing, maybe for the first time in your life.

I've always believed that if everyone in a church tithed, that church could change the world. God gives us individually enough to give enough to do all God wants to do. When He wants to do more, He gives everyone more to give... but, of course, that only works if people are giving a proportion of what God gives them... I believe God wants to do great things at Mt. Hope and wants funds for those great things to be funneled through YOU – if you allow it – if you let it happen – if you will

---

This sermon is an adaptation of a sermon written by Rev. Rick Gillespie-Mobley of New Life Community Church, PCUSA.

SMALL TALK

Deuteronomy 8:6-14,18 and John 10:7-10

For the LORD your God is bringing you into a good land—a land with streams and pools of water, with springs flowing in the valleys and hills; ⁸ a land with wheat and barley, vines and fig trees, pomegranates, olive oil and honey; ⁹ a land where bread will not be scarce and you will lack nothing; a land where the rocks are iron and you can dig copper out of the hills.

Deuteronomy 8:7-9

I am fascinated by words and how many of them there are in the world. I love to read, and am often amazed at how an author can use words in such a descriptive way that I feel as though I am in the scene myself. I can see the colors of the walls, I can feel the texture of the sofa. I can smell the stale tell-tale aroma of a Cuban cigar... And I'm pretty sure I'd never be able to write like that – certainly not for 2-300 pages. And if I'm not reading a novel, but a non-fiction book, I am amazed at how an author can take ONE basic concept and talk about it in an interesting way for 120,000 words...

And listen to the radio. Talk show hosts talk endlessly to me about nothing in particular, just rambling on and on about whatever comes to their minds – and I sometimes realize that there is nobody in the room with them. They are talking into a microphone without any kind of visual feedback to let them know if they are saying anything worthwhile or are boring their audience to death. Really quite amazing.

Then there is small talk. We all do it. We say things like, "How are you?" Sometimes we really want to know, but usually it's more of a greeting than it is a legitimate question. If the person is a new acquaintance, we'll maybe ask "What's your name?" or "What do you do?" Not bad questions to begin to get to know someone. Have you ever noticed, though, how quickly you forget the answer? Maybe you really didn't want to know in the first place. You were just making "small talk..."

But today is Heritage Sunday and I want to ask those "small talk" questions in a very serious manner...

How are you? Really. If you get beyond the, "I'm fine, thank you" response. What is the answer to that question. ...How are you?

Think about it for a moment. Usually you first think about your physical being. Maybe you feel aches and pains this morning. Maybe you feel chilly or too warm. Maybe you really do feel just fine. I hope so. ...But - How are you? How are you in the deeper sense? How are you doing emotionally? Is your life a mess? Do you feel stressed? Do you feel unloved? Do you feel that life stinks? How did you get there? How will you get to feeling better?

How are you intellectually? Do you feel sharp and ready to think about things or have those wonderful times of mental stimulation you had when you were young – ideas coming and changing so quickly – optimism and hope and expectation – have they been gone so long you hardly remember what it was like? Do you feel "dull" when topics of discussion or topics requiring thinking come along?

And, of course, how are you spiritually? (have you noticed that this sermon is mostly being preached inside your own head and not from the pulpit?) When is the last time you really felt the presence of God in your life? Where did that go? Might it be because you haven't been reading the scriptures (you've been a Christian and church-goer for so many years that there isn't anything new in it for you...). You haven't been leaning on God for your daily living. How is your prayer life? How is your devotional life? How is your church attendance? ... An old proverb suggests that if God seems far away, it isn't He who has moved... What do you think you might do to get back into a fresh and vital relationship with Jesus?

Being a Christian is a lot like being married. You settle into a pattern after a while. The love is still there but not the passion as it once was. But in the marriage you talk and you share your goals and fears and hopes and resentments... God is there to listen, too. God wants to know – How are you?

Second small-talk question: What's your name? Sure you can say "Steve" or "John" or "Sarah" or "Wendy" or whatever, but, again, that's just small talk. Those names are what your mother and father gave you when you were born. But you have other, more important names, too. Some of you are named "Dad" or "Mom" or "Grandpa" or "Grandma" or

"Aunt" or "Cousin" or "Best Friend." Those are your best and most important names...

But you are also called by the name of Christ. Does anyone know that? Even if you don't say it out loud, people around you ought to be able to figure it out pretty quickly.

Tuesday we were discussing, in our morning Bible Study, various things and we mentioned that if you are a group of people, invariable you will know in a relatively short time who might be Jewish. A Jew somehow let's others know. It has nothing to do with physical appearance nor even a "Jewish" name. Often the person will come out and make the clear statement, "I'm Jewish, so..." And I asked whether we, in that same group, would be recognized as committed Christians – as followers of Jesus Christ – as sons or daughters of the Ruler of the universe – as people who follow Christian morals and ethics and Jesus' teachings and who are known for our loving attitudes toward others... Who are you? What is your name?

And, within the Christian world, we are named "Congregationalist." No doubt you have been asked what that means. I am constantly, of course. "You're a Congregational minister? Is that a Christian denomination? Do you follow the Bible?"

My first response is to tell them all about the Pilgrims and the Mayflower and tell them that we are the spiritual descendents of them. But I've stopped doing that. People glaze over and *still* think we must be some kind of cult. Why would *anyone* want to be associated with such old-fashioned kinds of people? Were the Pilgrims even Christians?

Now I tell them that a Congregationalist is almost any Christian in any church if you were somehoe able to take off his/her denominational dressing. You see, all denominations have a certain doctrine that members agree to – or at least they SAY they agree to. But in reality, they insist on thinking for themselves. They insist on reading the scriptures and applying it to their own lives as the Spirit of God leads them. THAT is Congregationalism. We hold that people ought to be allowed to think for themselves, to be lead by God alone, to figure out for themselves exactly what the Bible is saying to them without some over-educated preacher or some denominational honcho insisting that he or the denomination alone has a lock on the truth. We – like YOU – believe the Word of God is an actively alive document that the Holy Spirit uses to guide each of us in His own way.

So – "Who are you? What is your name?" It doesn't have to be small talk.

"What do you do?"

Sure, you can say you're a carpenter or an engineer or a teacher or a factory worker or a bus driver – and those may be accurate. But what DO you do in your real – non-professional – life?

Have you ever noticed that all of us have multiple personalities? We are one person at work and another at home and yet another at church and still another when we are at the shopping mall. You can figure out appropriate living for each of those, but I'm concerned, of course, with what you do as a Christian and as a church member.

Some people will come to worship on a Sunday morning and sing the songs and pray the prayers and shake hands with a few people around them and then go home satisfied. That's fine. IF that does it for them. That doesn't seem like a very substantial diet of spiritual nourishment to me, but I guess there are skinny Christians and bulky ones. Nothing wrong with that.

But I've got to say, what I give you on a Sunday morning is a small portion of all God has for you. What the choir does is just a fraction of the inspiration God wants to thrill you with. The scripture lessons are just a sentence or two of all God has to teach you. The prayers are a minimal connection with God that He wants to have.

To DO what God wants you to do and to BECOME what God wants you to become is the goal. It should be what you DO in life. That means being involved with God in the morning when you get up – "Good morning, God. Thank you for another day. Would you help me in all I have to do. I have to …. and … and … Help me to always know you're with me." It means being involved with God when you go through your day, "God, that was pretty neat. I didn't expect…(such and such to happen)." "God, thank you for letting me keep my temper with that customer…" "God, this traffic is making me crazy. Give me patience…." It means being involved with God at home: "Hey, let's go to Songs and Silence tonight…" or "Did you sign up for that FIC group thing?" or "I think we ought to start a family devotional time. I'm going to buy one of those devotional guides and we'll do it, as a family, every evening at the kid's bedtime."

It means interacting with others about your faith. "Do you know what our minister said Sunday?…" "No. I'm afraid that's not something I want to be involved with. As a Christian, I'm not sure it is appropriate." "How about coming with me to church next Sunday?" "Why do I go to church? I'll tell you. It's mostly about my relationship with God…"

How are you this morning? God can make you better. He can give you physical strength, emotional energy, intellectual stimulation. He can give you spiritual life such that people will SEE Christ in you.

Who are you today? You're more than just your name. You are a child of God. You are loved. You are a Congregationalist who is seeking God's truth. You are a being created to go on living throughout eternity!

What do you do? Life needs to be so much more than a 9-5 job. Life is meant to be lived fully – the Bible calls it "abundantly." Are you living that way? You can. It will take some effort, but once that spiritual nourishment begins, your hunger for God will grow and flourish and you will become daily stronger in faith and in the joy of the Lord.

Believe Whatever You Want

Isaiah 61:1-3 and John 8:31-32.

If you hold to my teaching, you are really my disciples. Then you will know the truth, and the truth will set you free." They answered him, "We are Abraham's descendants and have never been slaves of anyone. How can you say that we shall be set free?" Jesus replied, ... if the Son sets you free, you will be free indeed.
John 8:31-36

I grew up with a very strong Church background – like many of you. I went to Sunday School every Sunday without fail – there were even several years when I got a little gold pin for perfect attendance. I wore it proudly. I sat through worship after Sunday School every Sunday morning – often reading the Sunday School "paper" that was passed out each week instead of listening to the 45 minute sermon (The paper was something like our children's bulletin, except with stories in it as well as things to do. Believe it or not, I still remember two or three of the stories in those newspapers – they may not have been Pulitzer quality writing, but they spoke to the heart of a child and have lasted in that heart for a very long time.)

Then, on Sunday evening we'd go to church again for a couple of hours... Wednesday evenings was the children's programs/prayer meeting night. I went to that until I was too old for the children's programs. I tried out the prayer meetings, but found them intensely boring... and I really didn't like to get down on my knees in the pew, which was the custom in our little country church. On Friday or Saturday evenings was Youth Group. I really enjoyed that and didn't understand, until Justin joined the Mt. Hope staff, how much time planning those meetings took nor how much of a heart for young people those who work with youth have. I've prayed a prayer, thanking God for Wally

Relea and Ron Morehead and any other volunteers that helped out that never got much appreciation from me.

In all of this, I gained a pretty good understanding of Biblical teaching and a pretty good grasp of theology. When I went to seminary, I was already far ahead of many of the other men and women there.

The only flaw I can see, as I look back, was that my church was exceedingly legalistic (I'm sure I've mentioned that to you before). The rule of thumb seemed to be that if it was fun, it was most likely wrong for the Christian to participate in. Now, don't get me wrong, I had a lot of fun growing up. Playing baseball, going on hay rides, attending sporting events, going to the local fast food places with friends – all good. But bars and dances and bowling alleys and playing cards and watching movies – not so good.

"But," I thought, "if that's what it means to be a Christian, those small sacrifices are worth it." In fact, knowing that I was a bit "different" from all my classmates and that I had to make some sacrifices for my faith, gave me a bit of a twisted sense of pride. Clearly **I** had discipline. **My life** was headed somewhere that was pleasing to God. I didn't need all those "worldly" things. I was living life on a higher plane…

Then I went to college and was pretty certain that my "religion" made me VERY unique on the college campus. And, of course, it did. But nobody noticed or cared. "Schafer doesn't drink or smoke or do pot. He doesn't sleep around. He doesn't go to the clubs or do much that is fun… See you later, Steve." And off they'd go.

Quite by accident, I attended a Congregational Church one Sunday morning and heard something that changed my life. The minister was talking about Jesus and clearly, theologically, he was on the same wave-length as I was – except that he was talking about how Christian faith is not defined by what we CAN'T do so much as by what we CAN do and HOW we do it and that Christ's truth should set us free instead of binding us to rules and regulations and that true faith shows in our works far more than in our fears and restrictions.

I had never heard anything like that Congregational sermon in my life. I would have recognized pretty quickly a low view of Christ or the scriptures or a sloppy theology. But faith without the rules was pretty heady stuff for me… And it was that day, I have no doubt, that I became a Congregationalist.

Over the course of the next few years I discovered some rather disturbing things about Congregationalists. I liked the Pilgrims and the heritage. I didn't like the witch trials. I liked the simplicity of the churches. I didn't like some of the politics that went on. I liked the freedom. I was a bit leery of the idea of the covenant instead of a creed... Did they really teach that we could believe anything we wanted to believe and that that was all right? Don't you have to have a statement of what we, as a church, believe? How do you explain something like that to someone else?

My disquiet of 35 years ago is not uncommon among Congregationalists yet today. How DO you tell people wrapped up in doctrine and bound by creeds and committed to walking the narrow way, that you aren't without seeming like some flaming liberal or sounding like "Congregationalism" is some kind of cult? How do you tell anyone in any other church that the church member who sits beside you in your church on a Sunday morning may very well believe far differently than you do without sounding rather wishy-washy in your religion? What kind of a church would allow such liberty? How can such a church survive? What was I going to tell my mother, who raised me in such a different way?

So I did the wise thing. I went to the source and made an appointment to talk to the minister. He told me that, in some things I was exactly right, but in at least one major point I totally missed the Congregational concept (He couldn't tell me what I was going to tell my mother – each of us are on our own in that regard).

He said that, when it comes to worship, WORSHIP is the thing that most pleases God in all of His creation. WORSHIP, in all and every form, is the very purpose of man's existence (he quoted the Westminster Catechism's first question and answer: "What is the chief purpose of man?" Answer: "To glorify God and enjoy Him forever.") Worship, he said, was never intended to be a place where we agree or disagree with one another. It is an experience that all Christians share. God loves it when His children, no matter what their race, creed, lifestyle, or social status might be, worship side by side in unity.

That was amazing to me. I had always thought that the purpose of going to church was twofold: First, to get those who were without faith "saved" and secondly to learn about what the Bible had to say. The strategy seemed to be that you pull people in through the music and the fellowship and the cute children's sermon, then you hit them with the gospel in the sermon... He was telling me that the sermon – the teaching – is NOT what worship is all about! Worship **IS** the singing and the prayers and the dancing and the giving and the readings. Worship is all about God. Certainly the sermon is a part of that, but the sermon is generally for the people. Worship is the people themselves giving and giving themselves to God. I had never heard anything quite like that! All week long God gives to us – our daily bread and our safety and our health and our homes and everything else... Then, on Sundays, for an hour, WE have a unique and wonderful opportunity to give to God. (That, by the way, is why applause is often discouraged in church – because since it is US giving to God, it's a bit like patting ourselves on the back for doing a good job – not all bad, but a bit odd).

Then he told me I was quite right in thinking that a church that doesn't believe anything – or that people who can believe whatever they want – is a pretty poor system. He told me, and I've observed this over and over again throughout the years, that Congregationalists tend to have the mistaken idea that they can, indeed, believe whatever they want. "That," he said, "would be no church at all."

While it IS true that Congregationalists have no creed to which we subscribe, you and I are NOT allowed to believe whatever we want (please don't ever tell anyone we can). But we are not, either, required to believe whatever someone else decides we ought to believe. Our truth comes from the scriptures. You and I, as Congregationalists, are required to believe THAT. Instead of the church saying "Here is the Apostles Creed. This is what we believe." Or another church pulling out it's six page doctrinal statement and telling you that "THIS is what our church believes and what our members are committed to?" Congregationalists pull out the Bible and say "THIS is the word of God. To THIS we are committed. It is my responsibility to read it and pray and seek the Holy Spirit's guidance in determining exactly what it means to **me** (not my church nor my pastor nor the person sitting next to me) and what it's application is to **my** life. That MAY come out looking and sounding somewhat different from my other Congregational brothers and sisters, but we've chosen to depend on the Holy Spirit's leading us, individually, into His truth and never relying on the dictates or creeds put together by man, at some moment in history, as our final authority."

I've got to say, it took me nearly the entire next to come to the place where I felt comfortable with that. Most of us WANT someone to tell us what to believe. We feel inadequate to figure it out on our own. That would mean that we have to think for ourselves – to be independent – to be, to some degree, "theologians" or, dare I say it, "adults."

For a long time I believed that, if this was the way it worked, very few people ought to be Congregationalists – that very few really would want to be... But I've discovered from you – especially from the various membership classes we've held over the years – that I had that wrong, too. The fact is that EVERYONE wants what we claim to have. People DO want to think about their faith and about what the Bible has to say to THEM. They WANT to be able to question and seek God's truth in prayer and study and come to an application for their own lives without being embarrassed that they don't completely follow the party line. They WANT to be on the journey of faith, seeking truth throughout their lives and not have it handed to them on a silver platter.

Like our Pilgrim fathers, Congregationalists continue to seek religious freedom... These days it doesn't take a treacherous journey across the ocean to find it. It only takes, eventually, to find a Congregational church – sometimes quite a journey in itself (we tend to keep our message somewhat quiet, for some reason). It takes the desire to truly be Pilgrims in our generation. To want to interact with God and God's Word. To have the courage to seek understanding. To have the compassion to know that others, too, are on the journey but not in lock-step nor at the same place as we are. To love God and the unity of His people more than our own opinions and beliefs. To KNOW that the way of truth is continually being revealed through the amazing, living Word of God.

If you are a Pilgrim today, you are on a journey of faith and freedom that most of the world will never understand – any more than they understood the journey of the original Pilgrims. But it is a journey that will challenge and renew your spirit and you will KNOW you are in God's will.

No, you can't believe whatever you want. But you CAN and MUST believe whatever God reveals to you through His blessed Word of Truth.

DO THE LOVING THING

Proverbs selections 14:29; 15:18; 19:11; 25:15a; and 1 Corinthians 13.

A patient [person] has great understanding, but a quick-tempered [person] displays folly... Love is patient.
Proverbs 14:29 and 1 Corinthians 13:4

Did you hear about the teacher who was helping one of her kindergarten students put on his boots? He asked for help and she could see why? Even with her pulling and him pushing, the boots still didn't want to go on.

By the time they finally got the second boot on, she had worked up a sweat. She almost whimpered when the little boy said, "Teacher, they're on the wrong feet."

She looked, and sure enough, they were. It wasn't any easier pulling the boots off than it was putting them on. She managed to keep her cool as together they worked to get the boots back on - this time on the right feet.

He then announced, "These aren't my boots."

She bit her tongue rather than get right in his face and scream, 'Why didn't you say so?' like she wanted to.

Once again she struggled to help him pull the ill-fitting boots off.

Then the little guy said, 'They're my brother's boots. My Mom made me wear them.'

She didn't know if she should laugh or cry. She mustered up the grace and courage she had left to wrestle the boots back onto his feet again.

She said, 'Now - where are your mittens?'

He said, 'I stuffed them in the toes of my boots...'

Patience – what a rare and wonderful virtue... And one of those things that almost always comes through practice...

Today we are beginning a fairly long series on a chapter of the Bible that I've probably quoted or read more than any other passage but on which I have never actually done any in-depth sermon. It's that thirteenth chapter of the book of 1 Corinthians – commonly referred to as the "Love Chapter." In it, the author tries to define what love is and what love isn't. Most often, when you hear it, it is at a wedding. It fits that context pretty well if you take it out of context, but actually it has nothing to do with weddings or marriage or even interpersonal relationships at all (even though, as I said, it fits that context just fine, too).

The church in the city of Corinth is having some major problems. Every person in the church is new to the Christian faith and finding that various different beliefs are causing some confusion. Paul writes the letter to straighten out some of their thinking.

By the time we get to the 13th chapter, he has already addressed divisions within the church where some are claiming a higher status because they became Christians under Paul's ministry or under Cephus' ministry or under someone else's. He has explained the devastation of the church when members sue one another, when they divorce, when they claim their "rights" as opposed to being humble servants, how they ought to act during worship times, and how the variety of spiritual gifts works within the fellowship...

Then he says, "Look, here is the deal. Let me give you the bottom line. There is a way of determining what is pleasing to God and what isn't. It's called 'Do the loving thing.'" Then he goes on to define exactly what love looks like and what it doesn't look like – and we inherit the "Love Chapter." We can apply it to our marital situations. That works very just fine. But the chapter is designed for *all* of our lives. What I'd like to do in the weeks ahead is to take each of the "Love looks like this – Love doesn't look like that" statements and explore them.

Paul starts out by stating that the best sermon in the world - even if it were given by Billy Graham or delivered by the angels themselves, is just noise unless it contains, at it's very heart, love. He says that even if a person could predict the future or know the mysteries of the universe or have the faith of the Pope – if he doesn't have love, he is nothing. He says that if you are Bill Gates or Oprah and have all the money in the world and make the amazing decision to give it all to the poor, you would gain nothing (although I imagine the poor would really appreciate it)...

Then he says, "Let me tell you what love looks like..."

The very first thing Paul says about love is, "Love is patient."

I've got to say, that wouldn't have been my first adjective to describe love. But then, as I thought about it, I realized that in each of our relationships in life that other person has the ability to absolutely drive us crazy if we don't just gut it out and be patient until the most recent episode passes... Patience. What an amazing quality to have – what an important part of any relationship... If we can't be patient while our spouse or our children or our co-worker or our neighbor finish the process of becoming what God is making them, we are destined to be intensely unhappy.

In Matthew (chapter 18), Jesus tells a story of a king who decides it's time to cash in his chips and retire to the mountains. He brings one of his debtors before him and demands repayment of the $10,000 he had borrowed. The debtor wasn't able to pay (who has $10,000 laying around?), so the king orders the man imprisoned and his family sold into slavery to pay the debt. The man begs the king to be patient (there's that word - patient) with him – he will pay it all back in due time...

The king thought the idea of being "patient" was an interesting one. Kings typically don't have to delay their gratification and no one ever asks them to... "I like this guy's courage – asking me to be patient! The very thought..."

He magnanimously decides to forgive the entire debt. "You owe me nothing. Go. Enjoy your family and have a good life."

But the man couldn't leave well enough alone. Suddenly he doesn't owe anything on his mortgage! He is debt free! "Life is good," he says to himself – "but maybe it can get better."

He had a co-worker who he had loaned a thousand bucks. If he could get that back, he could take his wife on that vacation she's wanted to have.

Unfortunately, the man's co-worker didn't have the cash on hand so he became furious and grabbed him by the throat and began choking him.

"Please – be patient with me (there's that word again)," says the man. I'll pay you back as soon as I can..." But he would hear none of that and had him thrown into debtors prison...

The idea behind the story is that God has shown us amazing generosity and patience over the years – (I don't know about you, but I'm sure I've tried God's patience on more than one occasion) and we ought to be just a bit patient and put up with others when they are getting on our nerves, too... Yeah, it's that old "Do unto others" theme again, but this time it has to do with keeping your cool when others irritate you or when things aren't going exactly as you had hoped or your loved one isn't operating according to your agenda... YOU'VE been there. YOU'VE been the one who has needed the patience of others. YOU have been irritating or late or dense or obstinate or wrong and SOMEONE has had to be patient with you... GOD has had to be patient with you. You've persisted in that favorite sin. You've been headstrong and refused to conform your ideas and priorities and beliefs to God's. You've thought your way was the right way or your timing was the right timing when God knew different... You and I have tried God's patience more than we can know... so we need to GIVE patience whenever we can.

Patience is such a big part of true love. Patience with your spouse is so important in a good marriage. When you live together there are going to be things that will drive you nuts. But love demands patience. We have a world that breaks God's heart with its disobedience and lack of regard for what He wants. But even in the midst of a world that breaks His heart, Peter tell us (2 Peter 3:9) "The Lord is not slow in keeping his promise, as some understand slowness. He is [being] patient with you..."

Do you remember Jonah. Jonah ran from God's direction in his life. But instead of God zapping him for his rebellion (or allowing the fish to digest him), He gave him a second chance.

But God being patient with us and us passing that on to others is only one reason for us to show patience to others. Perhaps another reason that rivals that one in importance is that nothing shows Christ in us less than an impatient spirit.

How often have you found yourself standing in the longest and slowest check out line and grumbled and complained and checked your watch and, when you finally get to the register, discover a pleasant cashier who smiles and greets you and does his/her best to serve you as efficiently as possible? Don't you feel a bit like a jerk?

Or when you sit in a traffic jam and whine and complain about the time it's taking and then, while listening to the radio, discover that an entire family had been killed in a terrible accident up ahead of you? You somehow know then that you are not the center of the universe as your impatience would have suggested...

Or how about when you do it publicly. Your impatience shows with your husband or wife in some way and your friends see your brusqueness or you being rude and you know that you aren't reflecting the Christ that dwells within very well…

If God's goal for us in this life is for others to see the image of His Son in our lives, then patience is a big part of that.

And a third reason that patience is so important: We make serious mistakes when we are impatient. That old saying, "Haste makes waste" is about impatience. How many times have we, in our relationships, jumped to conclusions without first hearing the facts? How many times have we opened our mouth and spoken when it would have been better had we been patient and listened? How often have we reacted emotionally to something without having listened and understood and, in so doing, have hurt someone?

Being quick with a response or being critical is a lot easier than being patient. But God wants us to develop it or it wouldn't be one of the "fruits of the Spirit" in Galatians.

True love is patience. Patience with your spouse, with your friends, with those you come in contact with and with the God who shows you love. Because, after all, according to the scriptures the first thing love is, is patient.

Christmas B.C. - The Seed

Luke 1:5-17 and Genesis 3:15.

The angel answered, "I am Gabriel. I stand in the presence of God, and I have been sent to speak to you and to tell you this good news.

Luke 1:19

What do you think 2007 will look like? It's hard to say, isn't it. The new year will begin in less than a month, but what it holds for the world is, for the most part, a mystery. In fact, it's even a mystery on the smaller scale of our state – What will the economic climate of Michigan do in 2007 or what is the employment outlook or the big news events? No one can say. Even in our own church it is all a bit nebulous. We can make plans and propose programs – we can EXPECT certain things to happen (like the construction of an activity center) – but, really, we just don't know what twists the year will take. And even personally – you don't know who in your family will become sick and maybe even die – you don't know if great joy or devastating disaster will come your way... No one has a crystal ball to see even into next month, let alone into the next 12 months...

I read this week about a man who was a well-known TV weather man in his city. He had a degree in meteorology and he seemed very qualified for his job, except that he seemed to be always wrong (like so many weather people). He became something of a local joke when a newspaper began keeping a record of his predictions and did a story that showed he had been wrong almost 300 times in a single year. Now, being a weather man is one of the only jobs you can have where you can be wrong most of the time and not get fired. But because of the bad publicity, this weather man WAS fired. He still needed a job and preferred to work in his field so he moved to another part of the country and applied for a similar job at another TV station. The job application asked him to state his reason for leaving his previous position. Do you know how he answered the question? This is what he wrote, "The climate didn't agree with me."

Niels Bohr, a noted physicist, has said, "Prediction is a very difficult art... especially when it involves the future."

This morning, we're beginning a little series of sermons for Advent that I've titled, "Christmas B.C." ...While it is difficult, if not impossible, for any of us to forecast the future, the Bible is packed with predictive prophecies.

Did you know that if you listen closely, you can hear the sounds of Christmas in the Old Testament? Written over a 1,000 year period, this first part of our Bible contains about **300 references to the Messiah that were fulfilled in Christ.** We don't have time to look at each one of these, of course, but I would like us to look at four of them during this Advent Season to help us understand who Jesus is and why His coming is so important:

CHRISTMAS B.C.:

- The Seed (Genesis 3:15)

CHRISTMAS B.C.:

- The Lamb (Genesis 22:8-14)

CHRISTMAS B.C.:

- The Place (Micah 5:2)

CHRISTMAS B.C.:

- The Birth (Isaiah 7:14)

Before we jump into our topic for this morning, let me make sure you grasp the significance of predictive prophecy. Most of these prophecies were written down more than *500 years* before they were fulfilled by Christ. This is no accident and is certainly not a coincidence. WE can't predict happenings NEXT MONTH, but the Bible can be pretty accurate predicting five centuries out!

Here is the significance: Lee Strobel, in his little book, "The Case for Christ," points out that the *probability* of just *eight prophecies* actually being fulfilled is one chance in one hundred million billion. That's pretty astounding. That number is millions of times greater than the total number of people who've ever walked on the planet! Strobel then quotes mathematician Peter Stoner who calculated that the probability of fulfilling *48 prophecies* was one chance in a trillion, trillion, trillion,

trillion, trillion, trillion, trillion, trillion, trillion, trillion, trillion, trillion, trillion! (Strobel, 246-7). And we aren't talking 48 predictions that came true. We're talking about nearly 300!

God knew Jesus was heading our way. He knew when and how and what he would be like and what would happen to him. He knew it all and told us through the prophets of old. Really pretty amazing stuff...

Today's sermon text is one that is not normally read during the Christmas season. It's only a single verse. Let me read it to you again: *Genesis 3:15* "And I will put enmity between you and the woman, and between your offspring and hers; he will crush your head, and you will strike his heel."

This is the first promise given after Adam and Eve ate the forbidden fruit in the Garden of Eden. It's also said to be the first gospel sermon ever preached on the face of the earth. Theologians call it the *protoevangelium*, or "first gospel." These words, spoken by God, contain the earliest promise of redemption in the Bible. Everything else in all the scriptures flows from this one verse.

Although you may not see it at first glance, Jesus is in the verse. He is the ultimate Seed of the Woman who would one day come to crush the serpent's ugly head (the serpent, of course, being the serpent in the Garden of Eden – Satan). In the process, his "heel" would be bruised and his body would be broken – on the cross. In short, this verse predicts, say theologians, that Jesus would win the victory over Satan but would himself be wounded in the process.

Because this verse is so important in the history of redemption, we need to understand something about its context.

1. (Time and Place.) We begin with the observation that this verse takes place near the beginning of human history. Adam and Eve have just eaten the prohibited fruit and sin has entered paradise. Their first impulse is to hide from God. Their second is to make excuses for their sin. Adam blames Eve and Eve blames the serpent. No one is willing to stand up and say, "I did it. It's my fault, and I take responsibility."

And suddenly the glorious Garden of Eden is not so beautiful anymore. The entrance of sin has ruined Paradise. I can almost see it – dark shadows fall on the ground as Adam and Eve contemplate what they have done. The smell of death is in the air. Under a nearby tree the serpent lies quietly. He alone is happy. He delights in what is happening for this was his plan from the very beginning. He intended to humiliate God by ruining paradise and now he has done it. He has shown the whole universe that God's great experiment would not work – that no race of beings could ever be trusted to freely obey God. Left to themselves they always disobey, even in paradise.

2. (Persons Involved.) As God surveys the moral wreckage of the fall, he immediately begins to deliver judgment. He begins where the sin began – with the serpent. Later he will come to the woman and then to the man, but he speaks to the serpent first. "You will be cursed above every other animal. You will crawl on your belly forever. You will eat dust all the days of his life...."

3. (The Bad News.) The bad news for the serpent is that there is no good news for him. God doesn't ask him what he did or why he did it. There are no extenuating circumstances to consider, no motions to file, no recounts, and no high-priced lawyers to argue the serpent's case. God simply pronounces his verdict. For the serpent, there is only a curse and a public judgment.

So what does it all mean? Three things:

1. It means, first of all, *Endless Conflict.* The verse talks about "enmity" between the serpent and the women – that means animosity or hatred or not getting along... Eve may have made a huge mistake, but she would never join the serpent's fan club(nor would her offspring).

But, of course, from that day to this, Satan has had a following, if not a fan club. Usually not overtly, but throughout history there have always been people who have done Satan's bidding... In every country, in every city, in every tribe or family – in each of us is the seed Satan planted in the human race so long ago. We see it in our own lives and it sometimes shocks us – the evil we can conceive or do...

In Jesus' day we see it popping up in Herod as he tried to kill Christmas. When Jesus grew up, we see it in the Pharisees who opposed Him and plotted to take His life. Satan was even able to infiltrated Jesus' inner circle, filling the heart of Judas with malignant evil. When Pilate offered to release Jesus, the bloodthirsty crowd cried out for him to be crucified, showing the evil seed that had been implanted in them so very long ago...

2. It also means *Temporary Defeat.* God then says to the serpent, "You will strike his heel." If you've ever had a heel spur, or pulled your Achilles' tendon, you know how painful that can be. We normally don't think about heels until we start having problems. But what happens? You end up on crutches, taking painkillers and perhaps having surgery.

When Jesus died on the cross, Satan "struck his heel" – he wounded but didn't put entirely out of commission... On Friday, just before sundown, when they took the dead body of Jesus down from the cross, it appeared that Satan had won the battle. But on Sunday morning, the true Victor walked out of the grave – alive!!

Sometimes we are "wounded" by discouragement, criticism, anger, bitterness, or perhaps by cherished plans that go astray, dreams that never come true, projects that never come to fruition, goals that somehow are frustrated despite our best efforts... This verse reminds us that the Christian life is not a bed of roses – wasn't for Jesus and we shouldn't expect it to be for us, either. Not only is there continual conflict, but the bad guys win a fair number of the battles. The evil one uses repetitive and excessive blows to break us down.

3. But there is, in the verse, also *Eventual Victory*. "He will crush your head and you will strike his heel." Can you see the difference. Bruising a heal (what Satan does to Jesus) is NOTHING compared to "crushing your head" (what God does to Satan in the end).

As the centuries rolled on, Satan kept winning victories but God kept raising up men and women who would continue the Godly line on the earth. Imagine this verse as the top of a wide funnel. When the promise was given, no one could have predicted the birth of a baby in Bethlehem. The "seed of the woman" simply meant that he must be a member of the human race.

But after the flood the line was narrowed to Noah's descendants, then later to Shem's descendants, and later it came to rest on one man – Abraham, the father of the nation of Israel. Then to his son Isaac, to Isaac's son Jacob, to Jacob's son Joseph, and then to Joseph's son Judah... Centuries later the line was narrowed to the house of David. Finally some nine centuries after that, the line led to the firstborn son of a virgin named Mary. What started with the whole human race had narrowed now, to just one individual – named Jesus – whose birth we celebrate at Christmas... and whose death we commemorate at this table today.

It was predicted from the dawn of time. Messiah would be born. Jesus would give his life. Jesus would live forever... and as we have His seed in us, so shall we. Glory be to God in the highest!

The basic outline of this sermon was borrowed from a sermon written by Rev. Brian Bill of Pontiac, Illinois.

www.ingramcontent.com/pod-product-compliance
Lightning Source LLC
Chambersburg PA
CBHW032018040426
42448CB00006B/656